She's Not All That—
JUST A GIRL FROM
Mississippi

S H A R O S L Y N B E N T O N

PAGE PUBLISHING
Conneaut Lake, PA

First originally published by Page Publishing 2024

ISBN 979-8-89315-316-3 (pbk)
ISBN 979-8-89315-300-2 (digital)

Printed in the United States of America

INTRODUCTION

Life holds no value without a purpose. This book is based on a true story of my life as a girl who grew up in a small town with limited knowledge of the world. However, my journey towards a clear vision was a masterpiece in its reality. Although many didn't teach me how to navigate different stages in life, the development path was a magnificent view. Ecclesiastes chapter 3 emphasizes that there is a season and time for everything. We may not get what we pray for initially, but if we believe, it will come.

Everyone has their own unique stories, dreams, visions, and goals. We may encounter challenges along the way, but it's up to us to decide whether they will make or break us. People always share their stories, but have you thought about yours? Are you truly living or just existing? It's normal to doubt your purpose in life, but don't worry. Take a step back. Focus on discovering your purpose and then move forward toward it.

Sometimes, determining your life's purpose can be challenging. If you are uncertain, you may need time to reflect on it. You may need to pray, meditate, or give yourself more time for it to become apparent. It's okay if it takes days, months, or even years to figure things out. You may be surprised that some successful people do not find their purpose until later in life. Personal growth is vital to breaking free from limitations and living purposefully.

Many people find themselves stuck in a job they dislike but continue working there because they need the money. However, one must consider the purpose of staying in a job that you don't like.

If you also dislike your coworkers, it can make going to work even more challenging. But why do some people stay in a job they dislike for years?

It is crucial to remember that everyone's situation is different. Taking steps towards finding a job that aligns with your purpose and brings enjoyment is essential. Understanding or acknowledging your purpose before you can continue to exist meaningfully is necessary. Please don't get too comfortable with the familiar or rehearsed words because they are all you know. Our lives are often based solely on what we were taught or have seen and experienced. It is not that you grew up wrong or did bad things; no one is perfect.

Everyone needs to find their way. Nobody has an ideal family either, and while some people may pretend otherwise, no one is perfect. Will you remain in the same circle all your life, or will you finally break those chains and set yourself free? It was hard to break for myself, but the lessons made it much more manageable as time passed.

I grew up as the youngest of five children. The behavior of those around me, including my family and friends, significantly impacted me. I was unaware of this at the time. I spent a long time feeling trapped in my little bubble, but breaking free proved to be the most difficult challenge of my life. Just because you come from a particular background does not mean you have to conform to it. You can change your lifestyle, but it all starts with you. Look in the mirror and take the first step. It's easy to talk about change but much more complicated to act. You can do it, or it won't happen.

Sometimes, we may doubt ourselves and our abilities, wondering if we will succeed. We often ask ourselves questions—such as, What if things don't work out? or What if I fail? These doubts can be overwhelming, and negative thoughts can creep in. However, the only way to find the answers is to take a step forward and try it. Rather than asking these questions, consider asking yourself if you trust in God to guide you throughout the journey. Do you believe he will help you achieve your dreams and take you far? Or will you go through this journey alone? It's okay to hold different beliefs, but in my experience, I couldn't have accomplished much without God's guidance.

Prayer has been the reason for my survival to this day. It's important to pray, as everything else will eventually fall into place. Life can be difficult and sometimes unfair, but we all have a purpose here. The events that unfold in this book are actual and challenging. To ensure the privacy of individuals, names may have been altered. The stages of this book will be in a different order, but everything will come together and make sense by the end of the book.

It can take work to keep going when times get hard throughout this journey. You should give the world the best of yourself instead of what's left of you. Imagine yourself at seventy reflecting on your life and asking yourself what you regret doing or not doing in your younger years. After talking to many older adults, I realized that living life to the fullest without regrets is crucial. Therefore, I started journaling during this time. Writing down my emotions made me feel comfortable and put me in my comfort zone. Writing became a relief for me when I didn't feel like talking.

It's normal to talk to family and friends about your problems. However, when disagreements occur, those secrets can come out or be used against you during an argument. Keeping things to yourself is okay if you don't feel comfortable discussing them. Some people prefer talking to others, journaling, keeping things to themselves, or seeing a therapist. Everyone deals with their emotions differently, but it's important to seek help when necessary and not evade problems.

Remember that everyone is human, and as such, they all have unique issues, problems, insecurities, fears, and bad days. It doesn't matter how much money someone has or how attractive they may seem on the outside; everyone faces challenges. Don't fall into the trap of thinking that others are better than you or that you are alone in experiencing difficult times. It's important to give yourself credit and not be too hard on yourself if things aren't going how you want them to. Accept your flaws, mistakes, and failures—nobody is perfect. Throughout this book, you will encounter the idea of embracing imperfection.

Regardless of the cards you were dealt in life, if you can find the light at the end of the tunnel, you can still emerge victorious. On this journey, you may stumble and fall. Some may even fall harder than others. When you fall, the key is to stand back up. If an individual stays down too long, it can be harder to get back up. Life goes on regardless of the challenges we face. After every storm, the sky clears up, and we witness the beauty of a rainbow.

Life can be scary, but taking risks can lead you to the best outcomes. Feel free to take small steps toward your future. Try to limit your fear and increase your risk-taking ability. Believe in yourself, even if nobody else does. We can train our brains to have a positive outlook and develop a strong sense of self-belief. Here is my story, and it begins with the different chapters of my life.

CHAPTER 1

The Journey Starts

On June 16, 1986, a dark-skin baby girl was born. My mother had five children, and I was the youngest. My sister and I were born just eleven months apart, so we were very close in age. My three older brothers were three, five, and six years older than me. Being the youngest has advantages and disadvantages, which I will discuss throughout this book. I will refer to my brothers as Brother 1, Brother 2, and Brother 3 in the chapters.

We were a small family, but my mother worked hard to keep us together. Although we grew up in the church, we sometimes strayed away. However, with God's help, we overcame even the most challenging times. My mother taught us about God from a young age, and she believed that "a family that prays together, stays together." I didn't understand the whole meaning as a child, but I saw my mother's strength and resilience. We were always known as a family of six, and my mother took great care of us.

Life is not always tranquil, but the wisdom of God has always helped me. We all go through good and challenging times, love and hate, and sunshine and rain. However, even in difficult times, God always makes a way. He may not come to us when we want him to, but he is always on time. The path of life is not always clear, and it does not give us complete understanding of this journey. Life is what it is; no one can live it for us. Unfortunately, we must live it ourselves.

Life is not always fair and doesn't come with instructions. It would be great if it did. But once you enter this world, your journey begins, and nobody knows what to expect. While the river flows and birds chirp all day, life never stops. Sometimes, you may wish to go back in time and relive some parts of your life, but unfortunately, there are no do-overs. We all prefer things to go as planned, but reality sometimes doesn't cooperate.

Many people in this world have varying expectations for their lives. Some may have been born into a life of privilege and luxury, while others may have experienced abuse, poverty, and other forms of hardship. Some may have grown up with both parents in the household, while others lived far away from their families. Some may have been in foster care because of their parents' life choices. Whatever our circumstances, we cannot choose our families; they are appointed to us by God.

I have to tell my story, as people often ask me why I smile so much.

In the past, I was in a very dark place in my life. But I always promised God that if he helped me overcome it, I would try not to return there. It was so dark that I could not see anything, and everything around me seemed black, even if it were right in front of me. I failed to see any hope of getting out of that dark place. I cried and felt depressed a lot, which took its toll on me. There were some days when I dreaded waking up. Yes, it's true. The smile was a cover-up for all the darkness I was hiding.

As I mentioned, nobody is perfect, whether they were born into wealth or not. If someone claims their life is flawless, it's best not to take their advice. Each of us faces challenges during childhood that may significantly impact our adult lives. Many people still carry the weight of their past stories today. While some can let go and move on, others cannot, leading to ongoing issues. Our experiences can either make or break us, but ultimately, only we can tell our stories.

Many people are struggling with mental-health challenges, yet only a few seek professional help. Therefore, it's important not to judge someone based on their struggles because no one knows their whole story. People are often quick to judge based on appearances or current actions. However, it's crucial to understand that we don't know what led that person to their current situation. Everyone has their unique story to tell, and it's up to us to take control of our lives and not allow others to dictate our paths.

My mother taught us many valuable things, including the importance of the Word of God and how to cook. Our childhood revolved around the church and the teachings of God. Cooking was also a significant part of our upbringing, mainly because our mom worked a lot, and we sometimes had to fend for ourselves. I enjoyed making spaghetti the most, which required only a few ingredients like tomato paste, noodles, salt, and a lot of pepper. The spicy taste of the pepper made my nose run uncontrollably, and although my siblings didn't like it, I loved it.

Our home stayed stocked with groceries. Mom usually bought quick and easy items such as chicken nuggets, tenders, fries, noodles, or breakfast food if we needed to cook for ourselves. Initially, my brothers started cooking for us when Mom was away, but my sister and I learned how to cook over the years. Cooking was great because we could choose instead of having it chosen for us. When Mom cooked, we had to finish all the food on our plates.

As children, we had to finish all the food on our plates before leaving the table. There were many times when we sat at the table for long periods until we finished our food. Eventually, my siblings and I devised a plan to empty the remaining food into the trash can. However, our mother caught on to our trick. My brothers then started flushing the food they didn't want to eat down the toilet. So if our mother cooked something we didn't like, we still had to eat it.

I grew up in a small town called Shaw, Mississippi, which had a warm and welcoming environment. It is located in the Bolivar County area, situated in the Mississippi Delta region. Although I am unsure about the exact population, if I had to guess, it was around 1,300 or more. Shaw is near Greenville, Cleveland, and Indianola, Mississippi, and is about two hours away from Jackson, Mississippi. Our town was relatively small, so we knew everyone who lived there. If we didn't know someone directly, we usually knew someone who was related to them. Most residents in our town were Black or African American, but we also had people from other nationalities.

Everyone in Shaw attended McEvans Elementary or Shaw High School, as we did not have a separate middle school. After I graduated, Shaw High eventually closed, and all the students merged with McEvans. Surprisingly, since our town was small, all the students could fit in at one school. Our school colors were green and gold, and we were known as the Shaw Hawks. We had an excellent sports program with many talented players representing our small town. Back then, teachers cared about the well-being of the students and would go the extra mile to ensure their success. Occasionally, they would even discipline us, and we were allowed to receive paddling as punishment. Parents were supportive of this practice.

Shaw High School was one of the best schools in the district. We had an excellent football and basketball team and also some of the best teachers you could ask for. Teachers like Ms. Brox, Ms. Tutwiler, Ms. Payne, Ms. Townes, Mr. McPherson, Ms. Smith, Ms. Davis, Coach Davis, and many more made Shaw High School a great place to learn. One teacher was known for asking students their names but interrupted, saying, "You don't need a name." Coach Davis was a cool guy and always fell asleep in the gym. Everyone knew where to find a student skipping class, and it would be in the gym. The gym was our hideout spot where we played cards, mancala, basketball, and other games to pass the time. I loved being in the gym because I could catch up on my homework.

One of my favorite times of the year was always homecoming. In the days leading up to the game, we had spirit week. Although I rarely participated, I love watching others, especially on "tacky" days. Students come to school wearing funny and impressive outfits that have you laughing all day. Even the teachers participated in the fun, showing their joyous side during spirit week. It is a time when everyone is in the homecoming spirit, and we all agree that this is one of the best times in our school's history. There is nothing quite like our homecoming.

The week seemed smooth, and everyone's energy was on point. This week was the only time teachers would assign less classroom work and homework. Students were busy working on homecoming projects such as preparing for the parade, decorating floats, making posters, etc. The band was practicing, and the dancers were preparing as well. The entire school was buzzing with excitement. Our energy level was at high positivity for the whole week. So, if you were planning to get into trouble, homecoming week was the perfect time. Students rarely got punished, as far as I could remember.

Our homecoming was always memorable, and it got better with each passing year. The parades were astonishing, with the band, floats, unique cars, and other schools joining us to make the whole planning process genuinely exceptional. After the parade, we would prepare for the homecoming game, which was the event's highlight. It was when we would see people we had not seen in years come home. Everyone would be dressed in their new outfits, with fresh haircuts and new hairdos, looking sharp from head to toe. Some people would not even watch the game but instead walk around catching up with old classmates, friends, and family. After the game, we would all head downtown.

Downtown was the go-to location for most people to meet up. They would be downtown if you couldn't find someone in the game. Roy's was where most people would go if they decided not to gather outside. The town would be bustling from Friday until Sunday night. Out-of-towners would usually leave on Monday morning. We always made sure to showcase our small town during this time. It was enjoyable, and we never wanted it to end. On Monday, students would come to school to share their weekend memories.

Shaw may have been small on the world map, but it had several prominent neighborhoods. I briefly spent my childhood in the country before moving to an area across the bayou where I grew up. In addition to this area, we had other neighborhoods in Shaw such as Bo Wright, Icehouse, Uptown, the White House, old and new projects, and areas outside Shaw, but still within our regions such as Choctaw, backwoods, the country, etc. All these areas formed an integral part of the Shaw community. However, even with multiple neighborhoods, Shaw was still relatively small. You could ride through the whole town in less than thirty minutes.

In our small town of Shaw, we were lucky to have a post office, police station, fire station, and library. We rarely needed to go to the next town over for anything; we had a lot right there. During Christmas, when I was younger, they used to decorate the downtown area with lights and put floats in the bayou. Shaw wasn't just a town, but it was our home. It is where we built our foundation and made memories that shaped who we are today. I'll never forget where I come from; this is where it all began. Growing up in a small town taught me to appreciate the little things. If you didn't learn from your family, you'd learn from your surroundings. The older generations helped to instill discipline.

When I was a child, the population of my town seemed huge to me, but now I realize it wasn't. Stop signs were common in my neighborhood, and I grew accustomed to them. As I got older, a traffic light came, marking a significant change in our small town. Riding around dirt roads and dodging potholes and rocks was a way of life back then. They didn't enforce seat belts, and we would ride without them. Police officers were few and far between, and sightseeing was easy with clear roads. These were the experiences that I cherished, living in the moment. As a child, I dreamed of one day leaving my hometown and returning to help build it up.

We used to live in the countryside before moving across the bayou during the first part of our childhood. Those days spent with my granddad, Johnnie Walker Sr., were the best memories I wish could last forever. The country life was simply different and indescribable. Our little town was about five to seven minutes outside the Shaw line, and we were closer to the Choctaw area. Choctaw, the country, and the backwoods were all close.

Despite being farther away, the distance was the only reason it seemed far. Even though those places were outside of Shaw, they were still within the same county and district. We all went to the same schools, and the buses would still come and pick us up. Usually, the buses would pick us up first. I assume this because we were the farthest away from the school. So we had to get up much earlier to prepare for school and not miss the bus. We would prepare our clothes, bathe, and prepare the night before. Sometimes, my mom or granddad Johnnie would drop us off.

Johnnie was not my biological grandparent. He dated my mom before, but I learned about their relationship later. Even though their romantic relationship did not last, they remained best friends. Seeing their friendship up close was a beautiful thing. They may have had disagreements, but it never affected their love for each other. Their passion was excellent, and they always had each other's backs. Whenever my mom fell short, Johnnie would be there to pick up the slack. He didn't just show love to my mom, but he also loved my siblings and me. I loved everything about his personality. He was a real blessing in our lives.

Johnnie would always pray with us, and we would anoint his head with oil before the prayer. The oil was a form of spiritual anointment. Before we started praying, my sister and I would sing. We thought we were good singers. Johnnie always kept a small bottle of oil nearby, whether in his car or pocket. He had a lot of things in his pocket, from peanuts to coins, wallets, pocketknives, pens, and more. Whenever he came into the house, he would empty his pockets and put everything in his hat.

The time I spent with my granddad was one of the best moments of my life. His love was infectious, and his positive energy and stress-free demeanor made me feel great. He used to take us for rides, and whenever we were with him, we felt like we were his top priority. We knew he would always stop at the store if we rode with him. As a kid, this was like a dream come true. We could go inside and pick up all the junk food we wanted, which was like heaven. Even if someone didn't come along for the ride, he would still ask us to pick up snacks for them.

If my siblings weren't home, I would pick up snacks for them. He would always ensure I didn't touch them, and they would be there for my siblings when they got home. He treated all of us equally and was fair in his actions. I would eat my snacks and wait for my siblings to come home and beg for theirs. My granddad always encouraged us and guided us in the right direction. Brother 2 and I were his favorites, but he cut Brother 2 off when he became disrespectful. My granddad had zero tolerance for disrespect, and even though Brother 2 apologized, it didn't change his perception of him.

As a result, I became the favorite. I felt more loved and received more privileges than my siblings. He would allow me to ride to Bible class at Douglas church and get more items at the store. Whenever my siblings did something unfriendly to me, I would complain, and he would handle it. My granddad was one of the best human beings on earth, besides my mom, dad, and siblings. No one could tell me anything negative about him because I wouldn't listen. He was like a miracle who dropped down from the sky.

He was quite the ladies' man and loved women. He was always well-groomed with neatly trimmed hair. He often left the top button of his shirt undone and wore his favorite black boots and hats.

He took great pride in his appearance and that of his family. He even cut my brother's hair when needed, so they rarely went to the barbershop. Although he was not my biological grandparent, his family still treated us well.

Growing up in the country was my favorite time of my life. It taught my siblings and me about nature and its wonders. The air was always fresh. The cost of living was low, and crime was almost nonexistent. It was a stress-free environment for us, with plenty of space, peace, and quiet. Our granddad owned his house and land, so we didn't have to worry about paying many bills. We could even leave our doors unlocked back then, but no one would bother us. Granddad had even left his door open plenty of times, daring anyone to try to come in.

During that time, the crime rate was low, and it was always quiet unless our granddad was mowing the lawn, having company, or on his tractor. I remember one day when our granddad was teaching my brothers how to cut the grass, and bees attacked them. The bees were aggressive, and everyone scrambled to get inside the house. My granddad tried to fight the bees off with his cap, but it didn't work. My brothers ran into the house crying, my sister was stung on the thumb, and my mom was stung in the back. The only one not outside that day was me, and I was relieved. Granddad entered the house with a swollen lip but acted as if nothing happened. To me, he was a strong, powerful, and well-built individual.

My granddad was always there for us, no matter what. He treated us like his own grandkids, and our bond grew stronger over the years. Whenever I needed anything, he would come through for me without hesitation. Even though he's no longer with us, I will always love and cherish him. His unconditional love was evident in his words and actions, and I miss him dearly. Living in the countryside with him taught us so much; his memory will live forever in my heart.

Letter to my granddad

Dear Granddad,

I wanted to write this letter to you, hoping it makes it up to heaven where you are now. First, I want to thank you for everything. Thank you for choosing us out of millions of others to love like your grandchildren. You saw something special in us and never wavered in your love for us. You promised to always be there for us, and you kept that promise. You didn't just meet our expectations; you exceeded them.

Granddad, thank you for always being there for me when I needed you. You not only told me that you loved me, but you showed me. When I moved to Atlanta, you reminded me always to remember where I came from, and I promised you I would. Even though I was miles away, we talked often. Whenever I came home, I always made it a priority to visit you. The last time I visited you in the hospital, I didn't know it would be my last time. I hated leaving you and Mom, but I wanted to do better and explore new opportunities.

Granddad, you always told me how proud you were of me, and that meant everything to me. I miss you so much. I think about you all the time. And guess what? Your name is tattooed on my left chest, so you will always be with me. Writing this letter makes me emotional. I never thought the day would come when I would have to live without you. Being unable to visit or talk to you on the phone when I come home is so hard. Now I must visit your grave.

But know this, Granddad. I love you, and I always will. The memories we shared will stay with me forever. Sometimes when I look at our pictures, I have mixed feelings. Some days, I cry, and some days, I smile. But you lived a great life and continue to watch over us. Save a seat in heaven right beside you for me. Until we meet again, I'll say I'll see you someday.

Love always,
Your granddaughter (as you called me)

*****

Moving from the countryside to the actual part of town was a different experience for me. While my siblings adjusted faster than I did, adapting was more challenging. In the countryside, our neighbors were a mile or two away; in town, they were beside us. Although it wasn't that far, it was still a significant change for me. The dirt roads in the countryside differed from the small potholes in town. I recall when my mom hit a pothole and damaged her vehicle, so it was essential to watch out for them. However, living in the countryside was all right. There were no potholes like that. I guess I was having a hard time adjusting to the new reality. Sometimes I wish I could have lived in the countryside all my life.

One significant advantage of moving to town was that people were always around. No matter where you went in Shaw, there were people everywhere. In the countryside, you would see your neighbors occasionally and a few cars passing by, but you do not expect to see people around. Another advantage was that it was only a short distance to the nearest store. We had to travel farther in the countryside for stores as few were around. However, there were also some disadvantages to living in town, such as nosy neighbors. They would know everything about you, from when you left your house to when you returned. It was shocking to have neighbors curious about your every move.

In Shaw, Leadway was a significant store that everyone went to. While we had other stores like the Johnson store, B & C, and Wild Bills, Leadway had a wider variety of groceries, school supplies, house items, personal items, and much more. The Johnson store was known for its amazing slushes, everyone's favorite. I walked there daily to get a slush and a bag of chips. My classmate's mom and dad owned the store, and I often saw her there helping. B & C had delicious hot tamales and nachos, which were quite popular. I could eat them every day.

Wild Bill's gas station was one of my favorite spots to grab hot food. Their potato logs and pizza rolls were my favorite, and I loved their hot and spicy chips. It was also a popular hangout spot for the older guys in the neighborhood. Whenever I visited, I saw someone who knew my mom or dad. The guys would be there eating breakfast or drinking coffee, having great conversations, and sometimes engaging in heated debates, especially during the sports season. It was always enjoyable to watch.

We also purchased from Step-Up Fashion and the Truck Stop. Step-Up Fashion was my mom's go-to store for purchasing our church dresses or for special occasions. She would buy everything from dresses to shoes, socks, hair bows, and even our school uniforms. My mom would always buy our clothes and shoes extra big, saying we would have room to grow and wear them for a while. However, walking around in extra-big clothes and shoes was weird, especially for someone as tiny as me.

The truck stop was where my favorite aunt, Martha, worked. She was affectionately known as Fluffy. She was a fantastic cook, and her food was always perfect. Many customers would ask for her, and they were disappointed when she wasn't working. Although we didn't eat there often, the burgers were juicy and delicious. My mom usually cooked at home, but the truck stop was popular. Leadway was one of my favorite stores in Shaw.

It was conveniently down the street from the high school and close to our house. Students would walk there after class; the owner was well-known in our small town. You could buy anything from his store, and he even offered credit for people to pay back over time. During this time, chips were only twenty-five cents per bag. A dollar would get you three bags of chips and ten cents of candy.

Going to the next town over, Cleveland, was not always necessary because of the convenience of Leadway. Plus, not everyone had a car to travel back and forth like that. Of course, you could catch a ride, but still. It was convenient, very convenient. See, if you had to go to Cleveland, you would prepare to be there a certain amount of time. When you are in a rush or need something quickly, Leadway is the option.

Unfortunately, the owner of Leadway lost his life during a heist. His death stunned our small town. How could someone who expressed so much compassion for our small community life be cut so short? This tragedy was a hard pill to swallow. *He did so much for our town, only for it to end this way,* I thought. No one was ever expecting this. Then to find out another victim died during this heist was devastating. The whole community was speechless. Hoping this was just a dream or something to make it better was an understatement.

Innocent souls! Our community came together for his homegoing; a visual took place in the parking lot of his store. This day was so sad; it was. No one ever saw this coming. Things happened, but sheesh, the pain, tears, warm words, and dedication filled that parking lot. Many placed flowers at the door. It will be a memory that we will always cherish. May he and the others continue to rest in peace. His store will forever be one of Shaw's spotlights.

You always hear about gun violence on the news, but never in a million years would I ever expect it to be so close to home. Not only was the crime close to home, but the accuser—yes, someone close to me! I never envisioned my loved one committing such an unforgettable act. Both families were affected. Families on the left planned funerals; the families on the right planned to visit their children behind bars. The emotions and disappointments were at their highest.

The devasting news of someone close to me and an associate was appalling. Very young! I was in a state of shock. Before this time, we discovered that this individual was related to us; we began communicating and got extremely close. We were in the phase of building a closer relationship. Knowing that my loved one was about to face one of the most difficult challenges in their life was distressing. So young. In my head, I wondered, *What were you thinking? Why? It was insensitive and wrong; I couldn't figure it out.*

Who am I to judge? You are the master of your decisions and must live with them. During that time, I cried for this loved one because I felt as though they had thrown their life away and would spend it behind bars for a long time. Not to mention, life was just starting for them. The discussions were widespread. The judgment from many was intense. The decision made was all we had heard about for months.

Grudges were held. Negativity planted, but life didn't stop. No matter how much we all hurt, life kept going. It did not stop! Those days following the incident were challenging. The chaos brought a lot of stress. We would get questioned a lot too. How do you move forward? How do you embrace the new lifestyle after performing this action? It was not me, but it was someone who I was building a relationship with and knew. So a war was going on.

My loved one made a huge mistake. Before this, we would have some deep life conversations. It was a period when they came to live near us. It went from conversing over the phone and minutes away from each other to this. Hearing the regret in their voice during our conversations was painful. Although they never admitted to this offense, the regret was there.

In life, you will mess up or make mistakes. Some you may come back from; some you may not. No one knows the real you, no one. It is not a justification for their action, but no one knows what battles others are facing in their heads.

Letter to my loved one,

Dear Love,

Hi, I am writing this letter to let you know that it's essential to stay positive. We all make mistakes, but it's crucial to learn from them and grow. Remembering that God forgives is also important, so making mistakes is okay. I hope you learn from this experience and can share your side of the story one day. Remember that I love you, and God loves you too. When life gets tough, remember to pray, as prayer can change both people and circumstances.

Keep working hard behind the scenes, and trust that God will step in when you need him most. I always appreciate our conversations because you help me feel better. Now is the time to focus on what's ahead rather than dwelling on the past. It's important to lose yourself to find yourself, so keep working on yourself and building a better future. Remember that I'm here for you and that I love you.

Signed,
Sharoslyn

*****

Matthew 6:14 states, "For if you forgive men their trespasses, your heavenly Father will also forgive you." No matter how hard it may be, you must forgive. You cannot reverse or rewind the damage when done. However, it would help if you learned from it. No lesson in life comes without a cost. The older I became, the more I understood this scripture. When I was younger, the thought of that statement was just an okay response, right? Now, it is clear as day. It is harder to forgive people, but forgiving is the best yet the hardest. How do you forgive others, especially those closest to you? It will take work! Not every storm in your life comes to disrupt you, but some come to clear your path.

We all have made some of the worst mistakes, including myself. Do I wish I could undo them? I sure do. I have said things I dreaded, proud to say then. Do I wish I could take those words back? I sure do. I am learning daily from all my life experiences. I am not perfect, and neither are you. Stop proclaiming to be perfect if you are not. I am a person who has messed up so many times yet tries to do better. I let my feelings overtake my thoughts, and my reactions get the best of me. I would react before thinking about it and speak before choosing my words.

Overthinking and overreacting were common for me. It was a huge downfall. When a person overthinks, this brings about stress, believe it or not. Overthinking can set you up for ruthless cycles that can be harder to break over time. Stress can affect your mental health seriously. It happened to me, not to mention overreacting. The situation can be as small as a dime, but my reactions cause it to blow over into a tire. Yes, my attitude was nonchalant.

My attitude was awful. Mom would tell me all the time that my attitude needed adjusting. Here was this girl, or young lady, full of anger but set in her ways. Where did all the anger come from? If I wanted to change my attitude, how would I? It was more challenging than one, two, three, or a magic pill I could swallow to make it perfect or right. That attitude was formed over time, over the years of disappointments, hurt, feeling left out, no support system, and so on. How can one change all that? Hmm, good question. Was I willing to change? *No.* My attitude reflected how you treated me. I was angry at the world it seemed like.

CHAPTER 2

The Fights

Being the youngest in the family, my mom always favored me as a result. My siblings would tease me about it, but I didn't mind. Sometimes, I would escape punishment for things that they couldn't. However, being the favorite child caused discomfort among my siblings and me. My mom relied on me to relate information about what was happening in the house when she wasn't around; providing this information to my mom made my siblings angry, and they called me a snitch. Sometimes, they tried to bribe me with my favorite snacks or toys, but it didn't always work.

Despite my siblings' feelings, I always felt loyal to my mom. She worked hard to provide for us as a single parent, and I wanted to help her in any way I could. Without question, the job would get done.

She could trust me to be honest and report any news regarding the household that she wasn't aware of. Mom always worked a lot; she worked so much during this time. Working was her lifestyle. Providing for her family as a single parent was always a priority. She worked two or three jobs to make ends meet, but we never went without food, clothes, or anything.

My siblings and I had different fathers. My sister and I had the same father, while my brothers 1 and 2 had the same father. Brother 3 had his own father, who lived out of state and didn't visit often.

My sister and I spent a lot of time with our father before he went to prison, but Brother 3 didn't have that same opportunity. Although he had his father to himself, he never had a close relationship with him. One time, when we went to pick up Brother 3 from his grandmother's house, he came running out with a big smile and several brown bags. It was one of the rare times he got to see his dad's side of the family.

When we were kids, we got excited one day while seeing Brother 3 approaching the car with the bags. We thought he had candy or other good stuff from his facial expression. However, we ended up disappointed when he opened the bags. We made fun of him for giving us pears, pecans, and oranges that were about to spoil in two days. Even though we teased him, we could tell he was happy to bring something for us.

Growing up, we did not experience a long-term male figure in mom's life. My mother did a great job raising us all, but a positive male figure living in the house may have been more beneficial for my brothers. Raising boys requires a father's involvement. Children never ask to be born, but it's the responsibility of the parents to provide for them. Raising a child is challenging, but having a support system makes it much less stressful and more beneficial.

When we were young, my mother wouldn't allow us to have friends over. She wanted us to stay in the yard where she could see us. However, my brothers used to have their friends over when my mother went to work. Our house was the most popular in the neighborhood, and everyone would come over to fix bikes, play basketball, and have fun. My brothers' friends knew when it was okay to come over and when it wasn't because everyone would be afraid of my mom. She could have been more friendly.

At times, my mom would act harshly toward my brothers' friends who came to our house. Her behavior was so mean that they started avoiding her. She would come home early sometimes, and if any of my brothers' friends were in the house, they had to leave immediately through the back door. We seemed confined, unable to engage in activities like other kids. It was disheartening, and I only comprehended its full impact later.

I recall one time my sister sneaked out of the house. She wasn't expecting Mom to come back early, but she did. Mom thought my sister was missing and contacted our pastor, her best friend, Mary Ann, and other church members to help find her. My sister wasn't missing; she was afraid to come home since Mom was back early. I could only imagine what she was going through at the time. Regardless, she knew she was in trouble.

They began praying for my sister. Mom even rode around town looking for her. Eventually, my sister entered the house, and Mom cried while hugging her. Mom thought that she lost her daughter, but not knowing this little fast girl snuck out of the house willingly. My sister didn't get into trouble that day. Mom was more excited to see her than give her a whipping like she usually always does. My sister lucked up that day.

We all have sneaked out of the house once in our younger days. Although I was known as the snitch of the family, I did not tell anyone in this case. For instance, I sneaked out of the house on Halloween. We were not allowed to go trick-or-treating, but all our friends did, and we didn't want to be left out. We collected a lot of candy, had a wonderful time, and enjoyed being out of the house. We made sure to be home before dark and not to go to any houses where Mom's close friends lived. If she found out, we would be in big trouble.

My brothers made sure we were safe while out and that we made it home safely. After trick-or- treating, we would go back home and count our candy. We would even trade candy. We would hide our candy under our pillow or bed from my mom so she would not see it. Even beforehand, we all created our lie to tell just in case we got caught. At that time, we knew to stick together regardless of the facts. We never got caught though.

Instead of thinking about toys, books, or kids' stuff at an early age, my mind stayed worried. We knew that our mother had to work. Yes, this we knew. However, her being away so much affected us. Her absence took too much quality time away, and it bothered me. Unfortunately, she had to do what she had to do. Many parents do not want to be away from their kids, but sometimes, they don't have a choice if they are the sole provider.

On the other hand, some parents rely on others to care for their children while working. I never considered this option before and only had one question: What about us? I never thought much about responsibilities back then. When my mother went to work, we had to stay with relatives or family friends. It was fascinating to see how different family members took care of us. Although I love my family, some of them could be a nightmare. Some only watched us for the money and didn't care about our well-being. They were only in it for the payment.

I am sure there's someone in every family who values money more than love. They can be careless or uninterested in your welfare but would still do it for the right price. It's funny, but you can have a favorite relative until you stay with them. The saying "You never know a person until you live with them" is so true. Sometimes, they look sweet and loving in public, but they are entirely different behind closed doors. We stayed with several people while my mother worked. One person even talked negatively about us while we were present; it was so uncomfortable. I immediately told my mother about it because I was the biggest snitch in the family.

My brothers would sometimes wake up early and go to work with Mom too. During those early mornings, my mother would pack food like crackers, Vienna sausages, beans, and microwave dinners for us. When she returned from work, she would cook delicious meals like fried pork chops, mac and cheese, chicken nuggets, fried chicken, and more. We adjusted since they were kind enough to watch us while my mother worked, and we had no significant complaints. Only some people made us feel uncomfortable, but some were pleasant. Some people would treat you poorly based on their feelings toward your parents or for unknown reasons.

Please don't say anything around me during those times because my mouth was like a river; it flowed. One day, while a family member was babysitting my sister and me, they cooked our frozen sausages in the microwave. Some people may like theirs cooked in the microwave, but it clearly states on the box to cook on top of the stove. Any who, when the sausages came out of the microwave for only two to three minutes, they were still white-colored. Have you ever seen food when it's in the defrost stage? It looked exactly like that; our faces twisted in disbelief. I thought, *Do you think I will eat this mess? I wouldn't even feed that crap to a dog, yet you give it to a human being.*

Guess what? Yes, the sausages somehow made it on the plates. My mind paused as I grasped my hand over my lips while staring at this meat. No, I didn't consume it, but I was nervous about it being served to us. That family member may not mean any harm, but I was clearly in a state of shock. That was food poisoning waiting to happen! Eventually, my sister and I placed the sausages in the trash, where they belonged the safest. There was no way in hell we would eat that crap.

Nevertheless, that was a challenging experience, but I still have good memories of it. I love my family and the friends of the family regardless. Although some may not have been as close to one another as they should have, they would still try to have each other's back. Back to what I mentioned in the intro, no one or no family is perfect. After that, I was relieved once Brother 1 was old enough to babysit us along with Brother 2.

I loved being at home and not having to go to others' houses while my mother worked. The only thing that I disliked about being at home was fighting with my siblings. Whenever those working days approached, I knew a fight between my siblings and me would break out. Those main fights would be with brothers 2 and 3 or my sister. Brother 1 wouldn't ever fight me because we had such a strong bond. For some reason, I couldn't get along with the other siblings for the sake of my life. Arguments and fights would come from pettiness things, which was very weird. When Brother 3 and I fought, I hated those fights.

Those fights were intense because he always fought as if he were fighting someone off the street. Of course, tears flowed with every battle, but I always fought back. As I was involved in so many fights, guess what? I became a fighter. Fighting so much built that anger toward leveling up. As the years passed, it was more challenging for my siblings to toss me around. With all those fighting techniques I incorporated over the years, my confidence level was through the roof. The more I was involved in a fight, the more strength and knowledge formed.

Since I was the youngest and smallest, I felt they bullied me. For instance, I could sit on the couch watching TV, and one of my siblings would aggravate me. While I was watching one of my favorite TV shows—*Saved by the Bell, Family Matters,* or *Fresh Prince of Bel-Air*—Brother 2 had a bad habit of just taking the remote control. He would never ask but take it and turn the channel. Boom! There came a fight immediately afterward! After experiencing the beat-ups for so long, I felt so much anger, especially since my mother or Brother 1 wasn't there to protect me. I decided to create a fight plan.

During my alone time, while my brother was preoccupied with other things, I would practice fighting in the mirror. Also, I watched a lot of battle videos on television. In my head, I knew that I couldn't allow any of my siblings to keep bossing me around. At night, while lying in bed, I would visualize beating them up. Sometimes, I would shake my head because I never understood why they would try to bully me when I was their little sister.

Creating a fighting plan for the next fight paid off. I was sitting on the couch one day, thinking it wouldn't be long before Brother 2 came into the living room to bully me. I was prepared for him that day since it was all planned out. Yes, as I was super young, making fight plans was a bit bizarre. My face demonstrated the anxiety that was running through my body. Believe it or not, that day, he took a little longer to come into the living room to aggravate me. I'm not sure if he felt the bad blood or what, but it felt like forever; nevertheless, I was ready and waiting.

Finally, he brought his freckled face chip tooth into the living room. He had been playing his PlayStation game the whole time in his room for the past hour. For some reason, he wanted to come into my space to irritate me as he had done for years. Again, I was ready and prepared for the foolishness on this day. The day came for me to stand my ground as I envisioned. As I predicted, the first thing he did was snatch the remote out of my hand and push me. The lick from my fist connected with his face and shocked him. Yes, I punched him dead in the face. He tried to swing and pull me off the couch, but I was quicker and rolled over. Constantly hitting him wherever I could, I didn't let off.

The adrenaline ran through my body, and there were no hold bars. The fight landed in the kitchen. Grabbing pots, pans, or whatever I could get my hands on, hitting. I was surprised that, somehow, I survived that fight. Yes, my brother was much older and still got the best of me, but let's say he didn't try me anymore after that day. All those fights changed me into someone that I regret. It came to a point where I felt I needed to prove myself always. Feeling like fighting was my only option to survive.

My siblings would never try half the bullying if my mom were home. When she was present, I always had that feeling of protection. Fighting my siblings always made me feel like they didn't love me. You would think siblings argue and fight sometimes, but be back cool in minutes. Duh, this wasn't the case for me. Although I wasn't fighting Brother 2 anymore, Brother 3 and my sister were still there. Brother 2 and I weren't enemies. He would do things to me just because he was older and thought it was funny.

Brother 2 gained my respect one day when he beat up Brother 3 for me. He picked on me all day when Brother 2 finally stepped in. Brother 3 locked himself inside the bathroom and was scared to leave. It was funny how he feared him but would quickly fight his sisters. Smiling ear to ear, all I saw was revenge. He finally gained access inside the bathroom and beat up Brother 3. His eyes blacked, but who cared? Not me. I gave no sympathy. See, my sister and I occasionally had a real fight; we would argue like cats and dogs.

No one wanted to fight daily, not even a real professional. I felt this way. If it wasn't one sibling, it was the other one. Now, at this point, it was becoming more exhausting—knowing that Mom or Brother 1 couldn't always be there had me with butterflies. I felt helpless because I had no one to help me during those times. I was so happy to grow up and gain some strength to fight back eventually. It was torture, no matter how you look at it. Even though we were young, my siblings may not have meant any harm. But what about the aftermath? What about all the hurt and damage it did to me?

We have all gone through a tough time at least once in our lifetime, which we must heal from eventually. Some may think it's not an issue, but later in life, it can become a massive factor like it did mine. Whether it was mistreatment or the loss of a parent, you need to heal in order to move forward in life.

No matter how happy I seemed, I had to face reality. There are things that were taken away from me during my younger years. I want to restore and rebuild to continue to move along this journey. No one may know the real me, no one. How many times have I cried? Have you been let down? Lost hope? Felt like you have lost your mind? Sad? Did you have thoughts of giving up? Cry behind those closed doors? Yet many are still fighting battles that no one has any earthly idea of.

Those childhood days are very crucial. You will learn a lot, experience a lot, see a lot, and more. The development of the brain plays a vital role during the early days. For example, having positive factors, stability, a relationship with your parents, and support can help nurture your positive outlook. Our childhood can have a massive impact on our adulthood. When childhood life is defective, this could lead to insanity. I didn't realize this until late in life.

As kids, we all had some of the worst little childhood names for one another as siblings. Everyone would hate to hear these names, and they even caused fights. My name was Blacky or Burnt Skillet. This name came about because I was the darkest child out of everyone. My siblings had either a caramel complexion or at least a shade lighter than me.

Being the darkest of the group, I always seemed to feel out of place. I always used to wonder why I was darker than my siblings. Growing up, I wanted to be light-skinned because they seemed to get more attention than I did. I figured they would leave me out on purpose because of my skin complexion. During arguments, this was a conversation for my siblings to take and run with it. So yeah, I believed for years that my complexion wasn't my topic of discussion.

My sister's names were Mold Lip, Gluey Bible, and Big Gums. She glued her bible together one day at church and never could pull it apart. Also, she had two small molds on her top lip. The molds were small, but we made that name terrible for her. The gums in her mouth were so prominent it was unbelievable. Her gum was so huge, but she had these tiny teeth. Every single time that she smiled, all you saw were gums. One thing about my sister is that she always loved to smile.

Brother 3's nickname was Blindy. He couldn't see anything without his glasses and was blind for real. During some fights, we would hide his glasses. In my voice, I'd shout, "YOU WON'T SEE TODAY!" He depended on his glasses. Once, his glasses broke, and he had to sit directly one foot in front of the television to watch. Yeah, his eyesight was horrible; it was an advantage back then.

Brother 2 was named Chippy and had a freckled face. His tooth got chipped in the front of his mouth, so we took that and ran with it. He was the only brother who didn't wear glasses. Although he didn't wear glasses, he had those freckles on his face. See, back then, freckles weren't a big thing. It didn't matter because we blew it out of proportion. My brother would be the one who loves to joke with everyone, but when the joke was on him, he couldn't handle it.

Brother 1 didn't have a valid harsh name because he never indulged in our arguments. On the other hand, when Brother 2 got upset with Brother 1, he called him "Bishop" or "Reverend." Those names came about when Brother 1 became a youth pastor early in his teenage years. See, that was the only thing that he could bring upon him. Since Brother 1 didn't bother us, Brother 2 would still be messy with him. He didn't care about him joking about becoming a young minister.

Brother 1 informed my mom that God called him to preach. At first, my mom wasn't into it until conversing with a close friend and member of the church. She stood behind him 100 percent. On second Sundays, the excitement of seeing my brother preach was everything to me. His sermons would be nice and short, straight to the point. Most of the time, he would write what he would discuss the night before Sunday. Once a month, our pastor, Reverend Wilson, would appoint him to minister and get paid. The days he would minister were my favorite Sundays because we would always go out to eat after church. Popeye's and McDonald's were the main two choices. Brother 1 always looked out for us; I was one spoiled sister.

Brother 1 was my favorite. He would never try to fight me and always protected me in any way. He was like my role model. Once he started dating, he was less visible at home. Nevertheless, the little time he would be home made my day. He grew up and had less time to spend with us. Eventually, he was expecting a child, and that crushed my heart. I felt he would forget everything about me once he had a child. I was so jealous when my first nephew, Jakieus, was born. He was getting all the attention now. Brother 1 eventually moved out.

Brother 1 was dating his high school sweetheart, Donna. Donna was always friendly to us and used to do our hair for us. She had such a beautiful soul. The news of her being pregnant at first was heart-breaking for me. Being the youngest, Brother 1 spoiled me. I knew most of the attention would be on my nephew once he had a child. That was not the case. When my first nephew was born, it brought us so much joy. He was such a handsome little fellow with a head full of hair that stole my heart. Mom would get him all the time, and we spoiled him. His other grandma, Donna's mom, would protect him. He had that contagious spirit over him and nothing but love surrounding him.

Shortly after Jakieus was born, my second nephew, Jacorius, entered this world. This was Brother 2's first son by his high school sweetheart, Zakedra. She was known to us as Kedra. One thing is for sure; she loved my brother. He played many games and wasn't ready to grow up, so they split and were on and off for years. Kedra was a good girlfriend and in-law to us. She always braided my hair. When my second nephew came over, I would agitate him; he couldn't stand me. He would cry all the time. One thing about my mom is, she went above and beyond for her grandkids. She always caught every beat. Eventually, later down the timeline, more grands were born.

The older we got, the less we fought, but arguments were more rare. Since Brother 1 was out of the house, it was up to my other two brothers, 2 and 3, to see over us. Then Brother 2 began to get into trouble and started acting out. He eventually moved out as well. It was bittersweet for me. He bullied me true enough, but I loved and cared for him. He was still my brother. Then it left us (my sister and I) with just Brother 3 to watch over us. Brother 3 began to rebel, and he was in and out of juvenile. Once, the police came to our house to pick him up, and he ran out of the back door. That was the last time

I saw him for a while. Now that Brother 3 was leaving the house, my sister and I were the only ones left.

Letter to my siblings:

Dear Brother 1, 2, 3, and Sister,

I am writing to say that I love and forgive you, guys. Also, I want you guys to forgive me for anything I did to you that wasn't right, let alone fair. Growing up with you guys has taught me a lot.

Brother 2 and 3, when we fought, I thought you didn't love me. The love and protection were what I needed from you guys. I felt bullied.

I had to choose between you and Mom when relating information. Although fighting you guys taught me how to fight, I never wanted to feel as though I had to fight my whole life. The wall of defense had me on guard.

Sister, I hate that we argued so much instead of loving each other more. We betrayed each other so much, but we rebuilt our relationship back later. Not having a stronger bond with you made me not understand the natural bond with friends or others.

Brother 1, you were my favorite brother. Thank you for not fighting with me and always protecting me. When you moved out, I felt like I lost a part of myself. There was no one to protect me. Then when you had Jakieus, I felt the love was gone. We barely speak now that we are grown, and I don't like that. I know you are living your life, but I am still a little sister and love you dearly.

Signed,
Your little sister

*****

With my brothers out of the house, it was quieter. Going from living as a family of six to just us was awkward. During this time, my sister and I argued even more. My sister would get on my last nerve. She would think she was right about everything and couldn't tell anyone anything. She was a know-it-all! She was more into boys and dating.

On the other hand, being a tomboy was what I advertised. I dressed and acted like a tomboy, always wearing tennis shoes and jerseys. I would get upset when told to wear dresses during those church days. You would rarely catch me dressing up; it wasn't my cup of tea. During my senior year in high school, I refused to go to prom. Yes, displaying myself in a dress was out of the picture. I'm unsure why I wasn't as girly, but it's okay. Eventually, the mind shifted as time passed.

When my brothers 1 and 2 left the house, there were certain occasions wherein they found their way back home. Mom would open her doors for them, but then it became unbearable. She wouldn't tolerate certain things. One thing that she disliked was wanting to act grown-up in her household, especially not paying one bill, wanting to be disrespectful, and thinking you would do what you wanted. Mom wasn't having it. There were times she put them back out for this type of behavior as she should. As the old people would say, "All grown people need their own." While at work, she instructed us not to open the door for them. Brother 2 would come by the house when he knew she was at work.

At one point, I felt so sorry for him; I used to cry because I thought Mom was being so mean. There were times I disobeyed my mom and allowed him to come into the house when she was at work.

I felt terrible afterward, but all I wanted to do was help my brother. There would be times when he would sleep in the car. At night, peeping out the blinds was a habit for me. However, I knew he brought a lot of this to himself. When he had a roof over his head, he took advantage of it and Mom. I was very angry with him for that. When my brothers decided to leave home, they had already completed high school and had kids. So returning home was a massive plus for Mom helping them.

The house didn't feel the same anymore. Even though we used to argue a lot, we missed our loved ones beyond words. It was hard to accept that they were moving on while we remained behind. At that time, I didn't understand why things had to change. I wanted everything to stay the same. I was comfortable with the usual routine and unprepared to face any changes. However, life is unpredictable, and nothing stays the same forever. So we must accept that life moves on whether we want it to.

CHAPTER 3

Train Up a Child

Before moving ahead in this book, let me elaborate on those church days in this chapter. Church always included a family of six—my mom, my siblings, and me. My mom instilled the Word of God in us since day 1. Church was our second home because we went there so much. We could have just moved into a church the way we kept going. No, we sometimes were there in the morning, noon, and night. If we were not at our regular church for Bible class or prayer service, we would visit other churches for revival, fundraisers, etc. Mom Dukes passionately believed in God; going to church, praying, and reading the Bible was a way to express her gratitude.

Church days were good memories. You could learn so much growing up around the old souls. Pastor Wilson was the only one who could grasp my attention while preaching. Have you ever gone to a church but got bored or not interested? You could learn a lot from our pastor because he preached so you could understand. The sermons were always on point, and his messages were clear. At other churches, you could fall asleep. The congregation was on fire when he added gravy to his sermons. Before him, we experienced other pastors, but he was always my favorite.

The church services would be every second and fourth Sunday. Pastor Wilson had two churches that he ministered at, but he showed love to both. The other church, Stranger Home, was down the street from our house, but Pilgrim Rest was in the country. We would ride down this long road full of fields to get there. It was the best church, along with everyone I associated with as a youth. Everyone was like family. Sundays were the day you got to see everyone. One of my favorites that my sister and I loved was our good buddy, Shirley. Shirley always spoiled us by giving us money; one thing about her was that she dressed nicely. We would be disappointed if we didn't see her at church.

While going to church, Mom taught us how to pray and study the Bible. See, although we read the Bible, the knowledge was not clear to me at such an early age, trying to understand who Paul or Peter was, what the disciples did, who the first to walk on land, etc. When we conduct study time, I honestly would memorize the Bible verses. Remember, my sister glued her Bible together, so she had to share with one of us during Bible time. It usually would be me. She and I would argue about sharing the Bible because she would try repositioning it closer to her instead of in the middle. How does someone who glued their Bible together try to demand control, you would think, right?

Mom would pray with us every morning and night, followed by a daily scripture that we were all assigned to read. One of my favorite scriptures in the Bible was, "Be still, and know that I am God." Regardless of anything that has or may occur, the Word of God will always stand. No, I do not pray or read the Bible daily as I should, but it will always be within me. At our daily sessions, I read Psalm 120, my sister Psalm 121, Brother 2 Psalm 122, Brother 3 Psalm 123, Brother 1 Psalm 124, and my mom would read Psalms 125–131. The reading sessions were not so bad; some nights, we were sleepy. No matter how late it was, we could not go to bed without reading our Bible or praying.

As time passed, through reading the Bible, we became much more knowledgeable. One word that always stood out to me was *faith*. That word appeared so powerful, yet I did not know much about it. You would hear church members and others use the terminology so much, but what was it in my head? People's favorite saying would be, "I had to step out on faith," during most of their testimonies. My mind was all over the place, just straight dense. What is faith? How does it work? Faith comes from the sky (just thinking aloud during those times). Then boom, one day, it all made sense when I finally understood.

The best example of stepping out on faith came when I over-heard and saw it one day with my mom. My mom just purchased her land and a new trailer house to put on her property. She always wanted her land and house. So many challenges came upon her, but she never gave up. First, her land was surveyed. After that, it was still an issue regarding where her land began and stopped. Since we all were new to the area, one of the neighbors decided to pull up her sticks from the survey. The issue was resolved promptly. My grand-dad was her biggest supporter, so he went beyond to help us.

From the beginning, things were not working out in Mom's favor. After the land situation, she faced another dilemma. The trailer home she purchased might need to be more significant to maneu-ver on the narrow street to get to her property. The area she was moving her trailer to had narrow roads that may not fit. You would think that she would have gotten discouraged. Well, she did not. Out of nowhere, she began crying and calling on the name of Jesus. About ten or more guys were trying to figure this out with my mom. Everyone appeared lost with confused faces.

Somehow, after all the struggling with the back and forth, they got the trailer one-third on the property. It got stuck. Yes, another dilemma strikes. Those guys, including Granddad, worked extremely hard; they even went to grab heavier equipment along with vehicles. The whole time, Mom never lost faith and continued praying. The trailer was finally entirely on the property. Mom cried and cried. She started walking around the house seven times while praying with tears in her eyes. When she prayed, that was her way of expressing her thankfulness to God. From that experience, no one could not tell me God wasn't real and faith didn't exist.

It was the first time Mom's dream of being a homeowner and having her land came true. Our house had four bedrooms and two bathrooms. Not to mention, we had a nice-sized yard. Mom brought us basketball goals to put in the yard so my brothers could play. Instead of running to others' houses, she would get things for us to be in the comfort of our own backyard. The first day in our new house was full of smiles. Everyone from my mom, sister, and brother—we were smiling. Brother 1 was happy because he didn't have to share a room. Brothers 2 and 3 shared a room; they had bunk beds. Mom had her room, but my sister and I shared. We didn't have bunk beds. We had a queen-sized bed that we shared. We felt as though God looked out for us. If it was an excellent time to believe in him 100 percent, that moment was it.

The Bible talks about how you must walk by faith, not by sight. Things may not be visible now, but you do not have to see it for it to exist. After that, I immediately started expressing my gratitude too. In all those Bible sections, I no longer felt impatient or doubted him. Also, you could not find me complaining as much about going to church. Since then, my mind thought that he took care of us. When you know better, you should do better.

Eventually, over some time, we did not conduct Bible sessions or go to church as much. We went, but the older we got, the less frequently we went. One reason was when Brother's 3 teacher called and indicated he was sleeping in class, it became one reason my mom slacked off going so much. Although I was more involved, not going to church as much did not bother me. 'Cause during the winter, it would be freezing inside the church. We would arrive early at church to light the heater. Even though we wore stockings, my legs would still be cold. We rarely wore pants as young girls. Not to mention, some of the churches we attended would not have those regular heaters.

Some churches had heaters that you light with those bricks. Of course, it took ages to warm the whole church. By that time, the service was over. You usually found an excellent position to stay warm when it was cold. If you move for any reason, it will feel colder. Here comes Mom, wanting us to stand up while the choir sings. On this day, we have yet to understand the reasoning behind standing up while they sing while everyone else gets to sit. One time, it was so cold Brother 3 did not want to stand, but she made him. Boy, was he upset. Shortly afterward, he got pinched, followed by the close-down eyes with the balled-up lip-stank face. If we misbehaved at church, we got a whipping at home.

Sparing the rod suited her perfectly. The kids of my mom's best friend's would make fun of us when we got into trouble. It did not matter where we were; sparing that rod wasn't a factor to her. I do mean nowhere.

Getting whippings all the time—I dreaded them. Not to mention, my siblings always felt that she got a kick out of showing out. They would talk about it in the car when she got gas or stopped somewhere and got out. We overheard one of her friends telling her not to chastise us for everything. I'm not sure if my mom encountered getting so many whippings from her mom, but wow.

Constant whippings did not equip us to be perfect, well-mannered kids. And to be honest, it was the total opposite. Whippings were a form of discipline in our household, for sure. These times were the one thing I despised the most. I would rather fight my siblings rather than get whippings. I despised whippings not because I was wrong but because they were the same all the time. So many caused a reaction in us all. Don't get me wrong, the reasoning behind it was clear and handed down from generations. Discipline is different in every household. No one could tell you how to discipline your kids. Many may have an opinion, but it didn't matter. Parents do what they think is right.

If you asked me, it would be questionable. Parents tend to pass along what they learned throughout childhood to their kids. I recalled when Brother 1 got a whipping with a belt from Mom Dukes. He ran into his room and locked the door. Mom was upset. She pushed the door open and tried to whip Brother 1 more. See, my mom always seemed to whip us for an extended period. I don't know why, but yeah!

Brother 1 grabbed the belt out of her hand and yelled, "Stop hitting me."

Mom ran into the kitchen. She yelled, "Oh, you want to be grown, huh?" and grabbed a knife from the kitchen drawer. Mom charged at Brother 1 with the knife, but he ran back into his room and locked the door. My sister was crying and yelling for them both to stop. Brothers 2 and 3 and I were looking stupid and shocked. We were speechless. My sister then proceeded to grab the knife out of my mom's hand and cut her finger in the process. Her finger begins to bleed. The blood was running like water all over the floor, on her clothes, and in her hand. Mom instructed her to position her hand under the sink and let warm water run on it. It wouldn't stop the blood flow, though. My sister got scared and panicked.

Nothing seemed to stop the bleeding. Nothing! We tried to apply pressure and all. So eventually, we had to take her to the emergency room. On the way to the emergency room, Mom informed my sister to tell the hospital that she cut her hand while cutting chicken. She was afraid that she made the worst mistake ever. She was super nervous; you could see it in her face. When we arrived, they took my sister to the back along with Mom. While waiting in the lobby, I worried about my sister and if my mom would get in trouble. After a few hours, my sister came from the back with her finger wrapped. She had to get stitches. After that, we left and went back home.

On the ride back home, there were knots in my stomach. I wondered what Mom would do to Brother 1 when we returned home. Since he was my favorite brother, Lord knows I didn't want her to put him out of the house or for them to keep up the chaos. So while in the back seat, I started praying for my brother. I knew that God answered my prayers because my mom apologized to my brother and sister when we got inside the house. She then went into her room with tears in her eyes. The house was quiet the rest of the night; you could hear a pin drop. Everyone was scared to move, and we just stared at one another.

We were all afraid of whippings in the beginning, fearful of getting into trouble alone. We knew that getting a whipping, no matter the wrongdoing, wouldn't be pretty—every single time. You would think that getting so many whippings would cause you not to do wrong, huh? Not at all. It wasn't the case. I believe it made my brothers worse. The more she said they shouldn't do something, the more they'd do it anyway. It could have just been them, typical teenagers, challenging her; I don't know. You would think that wouldn't be the case since they didn't like whippings, *not at all*. I believe my brothers received more whippings than anyone else.

One time, Brother 2 was getting a whipping, and he ran into his room and went under the bed. It was funny when Mom tried to get Brother 2 from under the bed. She couldn't reach him to save her life. He stayed under that bed for so long that he fell asleep. Mom was tired at this point but eventually whipped him later. There was no way to escape punishment time. Once my brothers got older, it was much harder to try to whip them. She had the strength of boys, but she could still handle them to a certain extent. It was different from when they were much smaller.

I recalled when Brother 3 was getting a whipping, and he ran straight out of the house. He didn't come back home for a couple of days. So yeah, we all dreaded the whippings. It would always be quiet in the house after one of us got a whipping. However, we would tease one another the day afterward. Don't get me wrong, I have had my share as well. While in the motion, my whole body would be burning. Afterward, we bathed that night to prepare for the next day. You can imagine how that felt, huh? Ouch. But the older we got, the fewer whippings we received.

Mom became less strict as the years faded. She may have become more patient, or perhaps she realized whipping wasn't always the best solution. Either way, we were cool with that. Sometimes, we could get away with certain behaviors we couldn't in the past. The change of heart, we loved it. I'm not saying that whippings were okay, but just not all the time. She raised us the best she knew how, especially while being a young mother herself.

Mom got pregnant with her first child, Brother 1, at fifteen. After asking her how that made her feel, she said, "I was a baby myself," her exact words.

A baby is having a baby. Motherhood doesn't come with instructions, so I could only imagine what was running through her head at times. Then she had Brother 2 at sixteen and then Brother 3 at eighteen, my sister at twenty, another sister who died at birth, and then me at twenty-one. A young mother with five children, all before the age of twenty-five years old. How was she able to manage at such a young age?

My grandma died when I was about two months old; I never remembered her. When Grandma passed, my mom took it extremely hard. A young mother with five children, all under the age of seven years old, dealing with the loss of her mother was traumatizing. Although she had others to support, her primary support system was gone. Not to mention, her mother was gone as well.

Nevertheless, Mom dropped out in the ninth grade. Now she didn't have an education, five children, and the loss of her mom, but she still puts on this brave face. Mom was heartbroken. No matter how much hurt she felt, life still had to go on without her mother being by her side. One of the toughest things in life is to continue on the journey without your loved ones.

She decided to raise and do the best she could for her children. Not all mothers would've taken on that formidable challenge, but she stayed in the race. My grandma had a total of seventeen children herself; three died at birth, from what my mom said. My mother only wanted the best for us and did what she could. Her sister, my aunt Barbara, taught her about the Bible. It was a huge factor in her and our lives. I don't know how far we would've made it without God. It was nobody but him watching over us all, and I thanked him all the time.

Some say that a long journey starts with just a simple step. The steps that you take today could change your life forever. But you still must show up and do your best. I applaud my mother for doing what she thought was best for us. Mom wasn't perfect, but she was perfect for us. Yes, she made terrible decisions throughout this journey called motherhood. I have heard her mention how she wished she could've done some things differently. Nevertheless, it's okay. We can never erase the past; we only move forward with the future.

Throughout this journey, Mom always showed tough skin, very tough. She was so strong that I gained that trait when bad things happened. However, later in life, I learned it's okay to be strong, but being too strong is unhealthy. Let me elaborate more. Sometimes, you can get to the point where you don't want to ask for help, thinking you can live life independently and be so independent that it could do more damage than good. In this life, I had to learn that it's okay not to be okay. It's OK to express your emotions instead of holding them in. It's OK to cry when things bother you, or you feel you don't have it all together.

We need to step out of our comfort zone. Remember that you are not alone. Forgive yourself for your past mistakes and failures. Most importantly, know who you are. Everything will fall into place if you trust God, which is what I learned the most. Prayer is what kept us and what is keeping us until this day. Mom dealt with things that she only knew. Her story was all she knew, and it was her story. Not to mention, my grandma had other children besides my mom to raise.

This is a true statement in life— "You have to meet people where they are."

It is okay to show your soft side. Never allow the world to change who you are or make you hard. Also, do not let your past or pain dominate your life. It can be a waste of your energy. All this can bring so much unnecessary stress to your life. This information is so important. For years, allowing the bitterness of others to steal my joy was tangible. Life is too short to be anything but happy. Reality is life, and you must take the good with the bad. You must love those who love you, not waste time or energy on those who don't. People who do not have your best interests will reveal themselves sooner rather than later. Believe them the first time. One of my downfalls was giving people more chances than they deserved to stay in my life.

For me, some of the lessons were taught the hard way. We pray for certain things, but it's hard to let go once God starts revealing. People would reveal their true selves, yet I allowed them to continue to mistreat me based on their status; it was not beneficial or healthy for me. Always forgive the ones who did you wrong, but never forget. Cutting them off while feeding them with a long-handled spoon is okay. Some people come into your life for a season. Throughout this journey, this is what I had to learn. No matter how much I wished it could be much easier, it was easier said than done.

Parents are critical. Kids rely on their parents from birth for everything, from protecting to feeding, providing, loving them unconditionally, and more. Think about those kids whose parents passed away and the grandparents or other family members had to step in. That wasn't the case for us; God blessed us. God blessed us with our mother to raise us; I am forever grateful for that. We tend to look at others' lives thinking they are better, but that may not always be true. You should count your blessings because it could always be worse.

Letter to my mom

Dear Mom,

I am writing this letter to thank you for all you have done for us and just to say a few things. When you started having kids, you were only a kid yourself. While having kids, you lose your mother. Mom, I can only imagine how that felt, especially having five children at twenty-one. You did what you thought was right, so I don't blame you for anything. I love you dearly. I forgive you for the lack of support and emotions shown.

Your lack of support hurt, but I knew you had to work. However, your absence hurt my feelings. Mom, you only came to one game during all those years. Looking in the crowd, hoping to see you, was just a dream. My siblings would bully me, and I needed you to protect me. Since Dad was gone, I was afraid of losing you too. There were plenty of nights I prayed for your safety. You meant the world to me, and the thought of losing you was driving me insane. You will always be my role model, heart, and, most importantly, the love of my life.

Mom, it's okay now. Your baby girl will make it. It is time for me to let go of my past; it is time to get help for all the past traumas. I trust God like you taught me because I know everything will fall into place. Though I failed a few times, I always rise again, Mom. My attitude was terrible because I had a lot of anger built up and took it out on the world. No more, Mom, I am letting go of that past. I forgive you. Please forgive me, and let's continue this journey together.

Signed,
Your baby girl

*****

My mom had always been my role model. The strength that this lady portrayed throughout the years was phenomenal. I know she had bad days, but she rarely showed them. All my mom wanted was the best for her kids. She did everything that she knew was best in her eyes. My mom was not perfect, but she was perfect for me. If I had to do it all over again, I would still choose her to be my mom. Raising kids takes a lot of effort. When I was younger, I never fully understood it. I was just on the outside thinking that I knew everything.

Those Church Days

Church days were so cool back in the day. Ms. Mary Ann was our Sunday school teacher, a great role model and my mom's best friend. She was like our godmother, but I truly admired her. Ms. Mary Ann taught us a lot within the church and was such a pretty lady. Her skin was flawless, and she always kept her hair done. To me, everything about her was perfect in my eyes. Sundays, she expected us to know the Sunday lesson and have our tithes and offerings. That was too much for my siblings and me. Studying the night prior wasn't in the plans, nor was saving our money for the church.

Of course, my siblings and I didn't read our lesson. This Sunday, she singled us out about tithes and studying. Although I was slightly embarrassed, it helped me understand the reasoning. Paying the tithes and offering at a young age was too much. Hmm, that was for the older folks. No, that wasn't the case! The money that my siblings and I received went to snacks. Snacks were way more important than giving them away or putting them into church. We didn't have a job, so why pay tithes? I didn't understand why, but things became much more comprehensible.

The following Sunday, she asked, "Who read the lesson?"

"Yes, *me*!" I was determined to show Ms. Mary Ann what I learned from her. Not only did I study this lesson in full detail, but my tithes were at hand. I saved the money I received that week. When she would ask questions, that blast of eagerness erupted. She smiled. She always wanted to see the best in all of us and would always utilize us throughout the church. My brothers were older, so eventually, they were in the older kids' Sunday school classes. As young kids, my brothers being teenagers, they still would find things for them to do around the church.

Our church only had an adult choir then but decided to bring on a youth choir. Every Sunday, the adults would sing. However, once they established the youth choir, the adults would sing on the fourth Sunday and the youth on the second Sunday. The idea of a youth choir was so exciting. I didn't know what to expect though except hearing the old, boring songs that the adults sang, which they sometimes did outside, ha ha. The adult songs were okay, but some were just old-school. It was time to bring in the newer generation to sing. In the first practice, we were arranged based on our voice levels. I was appointed to sing soprano; my sister, alto; and my brothers were tenors.

Shortly after joining the choir, I wanted to lead a song. I was terrified to say so at first. During that time, in all honesty, my imagination of being a star was present. Usually, I would always sing at home, in the car, in front of any mirror, etc. As that young child, singing was it. The first song I led was "He's an On Time God" by Dottie Peoples. This song was practiced and sung in the comfort of my home for months until I felt comfortable. My brothers and sisters got tired of hearing me sing while in the mirror. I felt I was on cloud nine with thoughts of singing like a star. The day was getting closer and closer for me to lead my first song. Each day was a burst of energy filled with excitement. Then it was time.

Now the energy was fading while the nervousness kicked in. It was supposed to be my moment. Although the day had come, time was moving extremely fast. Butterflies rushed throughout my body when it was finally time to sing, looking around with fear in my eyes. Suddenly, that excitement I felt all that time left me. Now all this time, you would think I would be ready. Seeing those people in church made me want to back out at the last minute. I just couldn't. We had been practicing this song for weeks, so it wasn't time for that. All eyes were on me when I grabbed the microphone. My legs were shaking so badly, but here was my moment.

The music began. I cleared my throat. Nothing was in my throat; I just did it. Before I even started singing, the inspirational voices took my soul. The congregation had already been clapping before one word came out. I even heard a few call me, "Dana," which is my nickname. The energy from that made me want to show up and out. I began singing, then something just took over my soul. I felt hit with a shot of Red Bull. You couldn't tell me anything. *Bam, the groove is there. Your girl is doing the darn thing,* I thought!

During the closing, I had to break it down, down, down, ha ha. The church was standing while clapping and cheering for me. I felt good. My level of cockiness skyrocketed through the roof. Tell me I wasn't Whitney; you couldn't crush my spirit. That moment was everything; the feeling needed to last forever. When the service ended, some approached me, telling me how great I did. Why did they do that? Of course, this was the topic for my family on the ride back home. My brothers dreaded it. My brothers were shy in the church, and all that attention wasn't it for them.

When we arrived home, the sassiness continued. On that highly emotional roller coaster, the decision that day was to lead another song. The other song was called "Long As I Got King Jesus" by Vickie Winans.

Now that this amazingly talented young girl was in me, the desire to sing more formed. The first song hyped me too badly, so it did not stop. The song had me practicing in the mirror like the first song. I would grab my comb or brush as my microphone. My siblings hated hearing me, especially since it was consistent. The words *stop hating* became my favorite throughout the house.

One day, during an argument with my siblings, it humbled me quickly. The words *you can't sing* broke my spirit. Yes, it destroyed my poor self-esteem. Even though I tried to act as if the words didn't bother me, they did. It discouraged me and compromised my ability to sing again. However, it didn't last long at all. 'Cause guess what? The following day, my energy level went back up. It went so far up it passed the sky! I referred to my siblings as "haters" from that day on. Finally, the day came for me to sing my second song. This performance was better than the first.

When leading a song, I would sing along with the radio. It will help a lot because if you miss a part of the song, the radio will guide you back or help you remember the words. For instance, one time, I was super nervous and excited, and at the same time, I almost forgot the words. The radio was perfect. The excitement of singing my songs would always be a memorable moment—all those years, I thought I could sing. As a young child, having the courage to get in front of many to sing was a huge step. Not only did I lead songs at my church, but also when we visited other churches.

As time passed, singing wasn't enjoyable for me anymore. That positive drive was fading. Sometimes, my mom forced me to sing. On the other hand, our choir director, LeeLee, always made me feel good about the song choices. Eventually, they would finally stop asking me to sing as much. The time came when the voice of a great singer wasn't near my vocals. All those years of singing, they made me feel that I could. Being teased by my siblings and youth of the church is when reality finally sunk in. Leading songs made me visualize that little girl auditioning. I would push out my lips, rocking my neck side to side besides being straight in that groove. Not to mention, walk around with this little sassy walk.

At church, they would have you feeling perfect about yourself and the day. Church was one of my favorite places on Sundays, especially when we formed the youth choir. The deacons would break out in the hymns and those powerful prayers. The moment was a fantastic time at church, including the altar call. The sermons were even good since we didn't have a boring pastor. So overall, it was an enjoyable time. For a short period, we were junior ushers too. We play our part in the church for sure. One thing is for sure, my mother was such a faithful member. She would show up morning, noon, or night; they could always depend on her.

During services, sometimes members or visitors would be allowed to testify. Testimony times were before the choir sang or the sermon. Yep, Mom Dukes would always be one of those people. There wasn't a time that she didn't get up. My siblings and I would be so embarrassed. For instance, this lady always started with aggressive talking, yelling, and then this ugly cry. Also, she would break out in this praise dance and wouldn't sit down after the music stopped. The Holy Spirit was something that she had, but my siblings thought otherwise. The time that she would testify, my siblings would lower their bodies down in the pew.

Mom wouldn't even need a microphone. She would be extremely loud to the point you could hear her outside the church. No lie. During her testimony, I would go to the bathroom. While in the bathroom, her voice would be so clear and high-pitched, as if she was in there too. I was immediately annoyed, and my eyes started rolling, my head shaking, and a stank attitude aroused. I blew and took deep breaths, hoping and praying she would wrap up her testimony soon. Then five minutes passed by. There wasn't as much talking in this world as I thought while listening in the bathroom.

My brothers always mumbled things under their breaths and would be teased by other kids for Mom's actions at church. For me, the biggest issue was not sitting down afterward. The pastor would be trying to go along with his sermon, but she was still up with the ugly cry. Her testimonies took forever; the more she talked, the more my brothers seemed to be dying on the inside. I recalled Brother 2 saying, "Here we go again," one Sunday when she got up to speak. We were young and didn't understand her praise or know why.

I didn't mind her testimonies. What concerned us was the extended length of time she would tell her stories. Not to mention, Mom would volunteer every single time. It is okay to tell how good God has been to you, but every time? Why not give others the same opportunity to say their own testimonies? I was so glad that they finally stopped the testimony time. It was the best news I have heard in all my life. I bet you any money she was one of the reasons why they stopped it. Sorry, Mom Dukes, but it's true.

Over time, my siblings and I got used to it and understood. Speaking more of the Holy Ghost, yes, she would dance anywhere. My mom wasn't ashamed to give praise or tell the goodness of God's glory. The praise flowed out of her mouth along her body. While serving him, she had a purpose. Yep, when we arrived home from church, Mom was the topic of discussion. If we didn't agree on anything else, that topic was one we all agreed with.

Maybe this was the only time we seemed to get along when we replayed Mom's behavior at church. Brother 2 would act her out from the beginning to the end. He would jump up and down like she did, talk precisely like her, and make those ugly faces. We would have a good burst of laughter. Every one of us would have our input in the show that day. Everyone participated in the show.

I remembered a time when my sister did the MC Hammer in church. I assumed she got it from Mom, but still got into trouble. Mom twisted and pinched her hand. Sister immediately started to cry. We were laughing because it was so funny. Wondering why my sister would jump up in church and break out with a dance was puzzling. I bet you she never did it again. It was a place and time for everything, and my mom took church very seriously.

She was one of the most dedicated members of the church. She served on the usher board and choir. She also paid her tithes faithfully. Sometimes, she even went out on Saturdays to help clean the church. Anything the pastor needed, he knew his selective faithful members could be depended on, Mom being one. There was a time when Mom got mad at the church and decided to leave. Later, she and my sister joined another church! I refused to join another church; I wasn't connecting with them. We were familiar with our church. Then eventually, she went back.

I never really understood why Mom would leave the church when upset. Then to join another one out of the blue was insane. I questioned if they made her that upset. No matter what church we went to, there was never a church like ours. You become more comfortable when you are used to the people and the surroundings. To go to another church, you must adjust accordingly. Get to know everyone, start fresh, and realign yourself to what you are not used to. Other churches had their rules that weren't nearly comparable to ours. For example, one church wouldn't allow you to sing in the choir unless you have been a member for some time.

Also, our pastor was very approachable. His way of delivering the message was clear. You could barely understand other pastors' words because of all the screaming. When we first left the church, I was distraught and disappointed at Mom. I was distraught, and there was nothing that I could do about it. However, I was glad that we made our way back over a short period. It was such a fantastic relief feeling. In those other churches Mom tried to be a part of, there was always one or two members who acted as if they ran the church.

Church is a place to go and enjoy God's Word, have fellowship, teach, and learn. It is a place not to gossip about one another. Hearing church members gossip allowed me to see people for who they are. They are human. They will talk about you and anyone else. They are human. They would smile in your face but add on to the gossip about you. After seeing some stuff, I realized that the churches are not perfect because the members are all *humans*. Again, when you are a human, you are not perfect and will sin and fall short of God's glory.

When your parents are deep in the church, people set high expectations for the kids. I often recalled hearing others say, "God wouldn't be pleased at how you act." They tried to see us through my mother's eyes. It put pressure on us a lot because I felt I had to be perfect. For a long time, I don't know why I thought people who attended church were perfect and committed no sins. Yes, that is what I thought, honestly. As a small child, I believed this for many years.

Just because someone goes to church doesn't make them without faults. Just because someone doesn't attend church doesn't make them a sinner. When it comes to God's Word, we must accept it on our behalf. A person can quote a lot of the Bible but still live in sin versus someone who doesn't and is closer to God. During childhood, I heard many say, "Only God can judge me." Many think you must go to the building to receive God's Word, and that's not the case. Yes, it's okay to attend church, but don't judge those who don't attend. All goes back to the part in the beginning when I mentioned no one is perfect, *no one*.

As time passed, the older children of the church ventured out. Whether it was graduating from high school, preparing for college, working, or whatever, our youth choir slowly parted. The youth and adult choir eventually blended. It was always different. The youth choir was gone, so we had to adjust accordingly. The adjustment was challenging; some stopped singing in the joint choir. Soon, we all went our separate ways. The choir started to get less and less each second Sunday. It was so disappointing because I enjoyed our youth choir. Nothing would stay the same forever though.

Once the older children left the church, it began to get boring. Let me tell you why I say that. First, I was less interested in attending at this point. Second, the adult choir had to start singing every Sunday since we no longer had a youth choir. The songs they sang weren't upbeat; they were more for the older generation compared to what we sang in the youth choir. I understood some of the songs of choice, but some weren't for me. When you are young, certain songs will catch your attention—the songs I was used to were fast and newer.

On the other hand, my mom did lead songs. Again, here we go. When Mom led a song, she didn't know how to end the song like she didn't testifying. The choir would be dead tired up there following her lead. Honestly, she didn't know when enough was enough. One time, the song was supposed to end after a particular part. Mom would sing the same verse repeatedly.

Those were the longest songs ever. Ha ha, she was long-winded at most of everything—the testimonies, leading a song, talking, giving whippings, and more. She had a unique way of handling things. She was weird sometimes, but she had her only little way, just like us all. I can sit back and laugh at it now. However, during that time, it wasn't as funny.

Knowing about God was one thing I loved about going to church. Again, the Bible states, "Train up a child in the way he should go, and when he is old, he will not depart from it." Even though I slacked sometimes, I knew I hadn't forgotten God's Word. There were plenty of times I had to rely on the Word of God to get through the difficult journey. If there's nothing else, I learned how to pray. Prayer is a unique tool that I have used a lot until today. I may not pray every day like we used to, but plenty of prayers are said.

The benefit of growing up in church was that it helped me feel much closer to God. Building a connection with the Word of God was a huge plus. Church would be uplifting, and sometimes, I could participate in communion. The first time I participated in communion, I was a lost soul just drinking and eating a cracker. I never knew what it symbolized truthfully; I just did it to do it. As a child, you would see the grown-up do it and follow the leader. How often have you attended church during communion and partake to eat? I will wait for those answers.

Communion would be this Welch grape juice and this cracker thingy that tastes like plastic. Sometimes, when we ran out of plastic crackers, we would use regular white saltine crackers as replacements. They would crunch them up into smaller pieces. After service, at one of the churches of my mom's friends, they would give us the leftover juice and crackers. My siblings and I would tear it up like the last supper. If you went to church, you would only have breakfast before church and be ready to eat—those communion days held us over.

In addition to growing up in the church, we got to fellowship a lot. Whether it was among our church or other churches, the pastor would get other pastors to come out and vice versa. Every time other churches came around; it was in me to show out if I led a song. Fellowship was a way to help spread the love and gospel across the platforms. Mom met a lot of people from other churches and became good friends with them. We would visit their house, and my siblings and I would play with their kids.

One family we knew from the church became a nightmare one day. We were building a relationship with this family, and one day, we visited their church. This family was enormous; the mother had twins and seven other kids. My sister and I were very friendly to them. One Sunday, one of the twins and I exchanged words because they were picking at church. I guess she thought I would be silent since we were at church. Well, she was sadly mistaken.

During service, we exchanged words back and forth. Once the church was over, the same energy lingered. When she got in my face, I lost it. I hit her in the face, and we began fighting. Yes, we were fighting outside the church. By then, my sister came outside, and the other twin began trying to jump me. My sister started beating her up. The twin who was fighting me tried to come, hit me, and run. I eventually caught her and beat her up again. They went and got their mom, but my mom was already outside by this time.

Church members had to step in and separate us. The whole church was outside. The twin's mom was so upset that she wanted to try to blame my sister and me. I was trying to explain that her daughter started it all in church. The twins had an older sister who was probably twice our age trying to fight me and my sister. She wanted to fight us, but Mom Dukes wasn't having it. The ushers finally were able to calm the situation. They got in their car and went their way, and we did too.

Mom wasn't even upset at us. Usually, when something like this happens, we get into trouble. Mom knew that we didn't create the drama. She informed us that next time, we should come and get her before something like this occurs instead of trying to handle it on our own. My sister and I may argue a lot, but we always had each other's back when fighting other people. No one could mess with my sister.

This fight at church was the talk of the town. Although this fight happened in another little town, it traveled back to our hometown and surrounding areas. After the chaos, we discovered they were known for starting fights. They thought we were weak, but little did they know I was a fighter. I was always up for a challenge when it came to fighting, no matter what.

Sadly, it was the first and last time this happened. Days afterward, I felt embarrassed. I knew better than to carry on like that, especially at a church. The church is the one place you shouldn't be fighting, let alone arguing. All this should've been handled differently and avoided. Of course, then, I wasn't feeling that. I knew right from wrong; I knew better. I told my sister that God would punish us for fighting at church, and the nervousness kicked in at that point. I prayed and asked God to forgive me and my sister and prayed for him not to punish us for our sins.

Since Mom taught us how to pray, I did plenty of prayers. My prayers were so sincere. When I prayed, things would get better swiftly. God may not have come when I wanted him to all the time, but he was always on time. His grace and mercy were all around us. Prayer is what kept me going even as a child. I thank God daily for allowing my mom to raise us in the church, teach us about the Word of God, and most importantly, teach us how to pray. Prayer saved me.

Here is my prayer to God

Dear God,

I come to you with my whole heart, thanking and praising you for it all. I don't know where we would be today if it had not been for you, who was on our side. Thank you for all that you have done for me and my family. I thank you for showing your grace and mercy even when we didn't deserve it. Please forgive us for all our sins that we have done and put them in the sea of forgiveness; remember them no more. Thank you for protecting us from all hurt, harm, danger, the devil's work, accidents, etc.

Thank you for finding a way out of nowhere and enabling my mom to raise us. There were plenty of times I wanted to give up, but thank you for giving me the strength to continue. Life isn't fair, but it's worth living with you. You may not have come right away when I needed you, but you were always on time. Even when it seemed like the end of the road, you would steer us in the right direction. I ask you to remove any hatred, evilness, envy, jealousy, or anger from my heart for others.

The ones who did me wrong, help me to forgive them and not hold grudges. I am ready to move forward with my life and leave my past behind me. It has caused me a lot of damage, but I am prepared to pick up the pieces to my life and live, not just exist. I can't keep living like this; I can't keep pretending everything is okay when it's not. I am choosing to walk away from the past and anything else, causing me to be at this complete standstill. Please continue to walk with me throughout this journey because I won't be able to make it without you.

Signed,
Your child

*****

Plenty of times, I felt God wasn't listening to me when I prayed. If I asked for something in my prayer, my mind would feel he wasn't listening. When someone did me wrong, I was immediately in a defensive mood. The reason is that things will always teach me a lesson whenever something goes wrong on my behalf. Sitting back, thinking others may be getting away with their wrongdoings, had my brain on ten. But I had to realize everyone had their own time to reach karma. Karma is real. You will reap what you sow no matter how long it may take.

Life has taught me a lot, yet I am still learning to this very day. Things may not come when we want them to, but one thing is for sure—God is always on time. Have you ever prayed for something that finally came years after your first prayer? Then, on the other hand, you prayed for something else, and it came in a short period? That is how life works. See, waiting wasn't in my vocabulary. I needed more patience. Throughout this journey, God humbled me. Life doesn't revolve around me.

Attending church a lot helped instill the Word of God within me. I also learned that not everyone attending church is perfect, and those who don't go aren't unsaved. For so many years, I held the belief that going to church would help you make it to heaven faster. Yes, I thought about this for years. When living this journey called life, no one has a heaven or hell that they can place you into. People will judge you accordingly, but God has the last say. Don't ever allow what people say to make you doubt yourself. Crazy, right? I have seen many people act so holy at church but turns to a different person when behind closed doors.

One thing that I came to realize was we are all human. No matter who you are, you are still human. People would put the pastors, preachers, bishops, deacons, and others who attend church regularly and highly as if they couldn't have flaws. Please don't be the pastor's wife or children; they look at you as the perfect person. Plenty of times, as a child, I would be afraid to do certain things because I wanted to portray myself as this "perfect" person for people. Did you hear that? I said, "For people." Acting like I was perfect was so stressful. You are living a certain way, but you know deep inside this is not you.

Even though I sang in the choir, it came to a point that I no longer was interested in it. However, I put on a face for everyone else; the older me wasn't intrigued. I thought I couldn't just say no; it may get back to my mother, or others would look at me differently. If the word got back to Mom Dukes, that would be even worse. During my younger time, it wasn't a choice for me. Unfortunately, we had to do whatever they asked us to do in the church. So saying the word *no* was out of the vocabulary.

CHAPTER 5

Daddy, Where Are You?

Parents are so important to any kid's life. One of the most challenging experiences in my life was having an absent parent due to incarceration. As I mentioned in this book, life was challenging, but this was when things fell apart mentally. In 1994, sadly, my dad was convicted and ultimately served close to eleven years in prison. The remaining sentencing was at the halfway house and on paper. As a young child, around seven years old, I was not expecting a judge to take him away from his children. I guess if you do the crime, you will serve the time. It is funny how a person could get more years in prison for selling drugs versus committing an actual crime.

My dad had six children; we did not all have that special bond. My dad and I shared a special bond. He would go beyond for his kids, siblings, mother, friends, or whomever. This man was generous. He held it down for everyone in his space. Before he was locked up, he had multiple vehicles and plenty of money while living his best life before things took a bad turn. If anyone knew my dad, he was always the life of the party and life in general.

Every summer, my sister and I would always visit him. No matter where he lived, he would always be available to get us or have someone to bring us for the summer. My dad always had different women; we could not keep up. One summer, it could be Keisha, Tonya, or Laura. The summer afterward, it may be Leisha, Jackie, etc. We could not keep up with the names. Each one showed us all love regardless. Unbelievably, women would be head over heels for my dad. Boy, if you saw pictures of him back in the day, you would be wondering what they saw in him. Sorry, Dad!

He was slim, dark-skinned, and looked a hot mess, but he was a straight-up flirt. His personality and the genuine love that he had for people was priceless. There was not anything he would not do for others until this very day. Dad would give you his last dime. You called Robert, he was coming. So many could depend on him, but I always thought others did not show the same love. Having such a good heart was his downfall.

One summer, I recalled my sister and I going to Bloomington, Illinois, and spending time with him. At this time, he was dating his now deceased wife, Jackie. We had an exciting time, but it did not last forever. Each summer was always better than the one prior, but this one set a record. One day, we were all riding the bikes when Jackie ran head-on into the fence. She was hurt. We were all riding bicycles that had something wrong with them. However, she grabbed the one without brakes. Yes, no brakes. Therefore, the only way to stop it was if you used your feet.

We all knew how to stop the bicycle without the brakes, even her. In this situation, we were riding down this steep hill close to the house when it all happened. As we were riding the bicycles fast, we did not expect a fence to be at the bottom of the path. Far to see, it was difficult to stop once we finally reached it. Her bicycle ran dead into the fence with full force. To this day, I always wonder why she did not try to react faster.

Boom, she hit that fence so hard her legs and knees were bleeding, and she had bruises on her arm and face. Immediately, my sister and I began crying. Panicking and scared, we called Dad. He wanted us to come back to the house right away. Those injuries were not life-threatening, but from the look of them, you would think so. People were standing outside while offering their assistance to help.

My stepmother stated, "I am fine, but thanks."

We looked as though she was not okay. Finally, we returned home with the twisted handlebar bike she was riding. The reaction over the phone with Dad was that he thought she would need medical attention. He applied alcohol and peroxide, followed by bandages with antibiotic cream. The healing process for her was super quick. The next day, she entered the living room as if nothing happened. If that were me, it would have my name all over medications.

Dad would always spoil us and give us lots of money. He also had other kids besides my sister and me. Throughout our lives, people could not face the reality of him being our father. So we went with the flow for many years. During that period, we later learned more about them. The summer was always the time I looked forward to each year. Spending time with my dad was the most enjoyable experience we had. The summertime was on the countdown each year.

In 1994, it was the last summer we spent time with him. Why did this happen to us? All I knew was we didn't get to visit once again. How could those fun summers turn into no-fun summers?

As a kid, there were things I did not want to hear because I wanted to have fun, see Dad, and forget about school for those two months of summer break. I did not understand why! Later, we understood why because of the possession of drugs. *What are drugs?* Hmm, that is what we were thinking at that age. Drugs were something I did not encounter or knew deeply about. So again, what are drugs? Why did he have them if it was wrong? Thinking this would only put more pressure on the brain.

Wishing that this all would blow over soon was an understatement. Not seeing Dad for the summers turned into one, two, three, and so on years. Feeling destroyed, my mind crushed, my heart broken, and no way to fix it! I was unhappy and angry at the world! I loved him so much because he was in my comfort zone. I could go on and on about this man, but you can visualize why this affected my life. As parents, the one wrong decision could hurt the ones closest to them.

After my dad received his sentence, we visited. Mom would take us once or twice a month, but sometimes more if it were near a holiday. Also, I recalled riding with others during a few visits. The road trip there was one of the longest ever for me. In my head, the words would be, "Are we there yet?" The first visit was the hardest; I was very emotional. As we arrived at the facility, my mind was clear.

The parking lot for visitors was near to the main entrance. However, once you entered, it was a different view.

In my mind, I thought visitation was getting out of the car, going inside, and seeing my dad immediately. The inside scenery was beautiful, fresh, and just clean. There were metal detectors, scanners, cameras everywhere, officers fully protected, and so on. As I continued to walk, the view was shocking. Yes! It was my first time experiencing this, so it was new. My movement was recorded from when I arrived until I exited the property.

After proceeding through those metal detectors, you would leave the main waiting area, go into another long hallway, and wait. We walked through several buildings and walkways before getting to the visitation building. Finally, we walked down this long walkway concrete building with many windows. We walked past multiple vending machines into this open space full of chairs, a play area, food vendors, microwaves, a photo section, etc. It was a sign that we were closer to seeing my dad.

As we waited patiently, other visitors began to arrive. Shortly, inmates began entering the opposite side of the room. The inmates would get searched before and after visitation. There were a lot of inmates entering, but where was my dad? In my head, I asked, "Did he forget about us?" Then boom. I heard his name; Robert A. got called along with his inmate number. After being searched, he proceeded over to us.

My mouth dropped, and my eyes got big. Boy, did my dad look different? He was not the skinny Black guy anymore. He had big muscles, gained a lot of weight, and his skin was much brighter. We ran toward him, and he kissed and hugged us. I kid you not; we could not stop smiling. My sister's gums in her mouth were already giant, but her smile lit up. Those glasses I had on were bigger than my face, but my smile matched them.

The love was there. I remembered sitting on his lap and enjoying this moment like it was old times. We eventually took pictures, got food and snacks from the vending machines, and just had great memories recorded. I prayed for this time to last forever, but it did not. After many hours of visitation, the time to say goodbye came.

My feelings were so in a bag at this moment. Reality hits! The time to depart occurred, and all the smiles faded. The sadness began to kick in.

Was this a nightmare? Why did he have to leave us again? Can we stay forever? The questions in my head made it worse. No matter how we felt, the time to go had come, and there was no changing that. I cried on the way back to the car. As we walked back from those buildings, it was breaking my heart. The tears would not stop. We were young, not knowing why all this happened to us. *God punished me for no reason* was what I thought. *Why, God? Why do we have to experience this when others have their parents?*

Over time, the more visits made it better. It didn't erase the feeling, but it eased it. The thought of knowing we would get the chance to see him made me smile instead of being mad. Once we got used to it, we could leave without becoming emotional. My dad loved us, we knew. It was not just him saying it, but he also showed us. Having him alongside us growing up just made life much easier. Without him, things were more complex. Seeing other kids with both parents used to make me sad all the time.

Parents' involvement in a child's life creates the most powerful positive impact. It helps a child perform better throughout their lives with school, sports, trying to be the best, and so on. Having parents who are involved enhances their achievements in more ways than they know. Studies show that an absent parent can hurt children. It is something that I went through. Although my father was not wholly absent, he missed out on a lot. The absence at my games, in a lot of healthy time spent—birthdays, graduations, etc.—was noticed.

After my dad went to prison, I honestly felt like my mom had more pressure applied on her, thinking it was not fair to her. Again, someone else's decisions could affect you and the people close to you. I was angry inside. My feelings were hurt and hidden. Yes, it hurt me very much. I had to live through it all, pretending that everything was okay. Many days and nights, all I wanted was my dad. We had that bond that was just unbreakable. However, even though he was many miles away, deep in my heart, I knew he loved us very much.

As I mentioned previously, Dad had other kids. One of my half-sisters Robin attended the same high school as us. For some reason, Robin would be so mean to us during the high school days. We would speak to her or try to be cool, but she would blow us off. We said, "Hey, sister," but she would yell, "I am not your sister," or "Get out of my face," and then laugh. It got to the point where I was scared to say anything when I saw her to save the embarrassment. Thinking aloud, I could not understand why she would act like that toward us when we were also Dad's children.

It felt like she had disowned us and didn't treat us like her sister. I felt like the wicked stepchild, alone, the odd one out. Robin was best friends with my brother's girlfriend, Kedra. So, of course, we saw her a lot. I wish we had a better bond growing up because it would have put a little ease on the challenges we already faced. Many people did not think Robert was our father, so we felt left out. It did hurt to encounter such behavior by Robin and others. I didn't choose this lifestyle; this was the hands dealt to me.

Puzzled for many days, I didn't know whether to speak or keep walking when Robin was within view. One day, there might have been a hi, yet other days, nothing or an attitude of rudeness. It got to the point where I became numb to it. All those years of embarrassment and hurt were the new norm. Many days, it would have been beneficial if we could only build that stronger bond. I was hoping that one day things would change, but it was only wishful thinking. Robin will always be part of my life; my love for her is pure no matter what happens.

All my dad's kids had different last names. My sister and I had the worst name, *Roach*. Yes, you heard me; Roach was our last name. Please don't ask why or how that name came about. I don't know where this name originated, but I wouldn't say I liked it. We would get teased a lot at school with that name. Since Roach was a bug, people would take that and run off the cliff with it. I recalled some of my classmates teasing us by saying, "Kill that roach," every time they saw us come down the hall or wherever. Some would say, "Raid," others would say, "There goes the bug." The names were hilarious. The level of creativity of the teasing was life.

That last name was just embarrassing, which was horrible. I mean, horrible. Who would sit around and name their child after a bug? There were no other names on this planet you could find. Why Roach? I would have just preferred Bug or Insect. My brothers didn't get teased because they were boys, but my sister and I caught the worst end of the stick. I never got mad about it; I would laugh it off because I eventually got used to it. Although it was annoying, it was expected behavior. Kids were only kids. Plus, we got used to the teasing.

I need to find out who even created the last name, Roach. In my mind, was it one day they saw a bug and decided to name their child that or what? I always wonder how that last name came about from so many generations. I would not like my turn to go to the back when we had a dentist, eye, or other appointments. Names called super loud when it was our turn to go to the back. Since it was difficult to pronounce my first name, saying my last name was familiar. My mom should've just named us after our dad's.

Mom claimed that she named me, and my name was in the Bible, but then Dad said he named me. The name of one of my mom's friends was Roslyn, and that's how the idea began. Then Dad said he created Sharoslyn. Now I just gave up on knowing this information about my name. From saying it was in the Bible to this or that, the case is so closed. My name is beautiful—that is it! I will live it to the fullest. My name has meaning, and it was meant just for me. We had a sister who passed at birth before me; her name would've been Sharoslyn. To know that my name would've been ShaRobert was insane. I thank God I didn't have to walk around with a name like ShaRobert Roach.

When I got older, I asked my dad why he didn't give us his last name. He responded, "Your mom gave all of you guys her last name."

But why? It should've been the right time he stepped in and said *no way*. Boy, I tell you the truth. Parents need to be mindful of what they name their children for future engagements. It is the name they must live with for the rest of their life until they get married or change it themselves. If I had known what I know now, I would have suggested a name change years ago.

Accepting that we have other siblings we are yet to encounter was nonsense. Like Robin's behavior, some of our family members did not welcome us for some reason. I recalled walking inside Leadway one day. We saw one of my dad's sisters, my aunt. My sister and I ran to her and said, "Hey, Auntie."

"I am not your auntie," she replied bluntly.

Hearing those aggressive words hurt our feelings so badly. We were young, and to be embarrassed by our family was insane. My sister and I both cried. Later that day, Dad called. We told him what happened, and he got distraught.

He talked with her eventually, but it didn't change how we felt. Mom could not fix it; no one can control how a person treats you, *no one*. The statement "No one will forget how you made them feel," is compelling. All these years, I can precisely relate what took place that day, word for word. As we got older, my sister and I elaborated on it periodically. I honestly wished we were closer to his side of the family than we were. Do not get me wrong, everyone was not that way toward us, only a select few. We experienced love from others. The one person who always accepted us and loved us unconditionally was my grandma, Mutt Dear.

See, Grandma had a pure heart. The love that she had for others was contagious. No matter who you were, Grandma would open her doors to you. Although she had a pure heart, she still didn't allow you to run over her. When people are friendly and loving, others try to take advantage of their kindness; she meant business. Don't get it twisted. The memories were beyond profound. After all those years, I saw precisely how my dad formed such a loving and caring heart. All her children—my aunts and uncles—had that gracious heart or loving spirit.

Grandma was always the glue to the family. I would spend the night at her house or always visit for many years. She always made me feel welcome. She cooked for and engaged with me. Some of my cousins would be over at the same time as me; we had fun. Grandma kept fussing, but it was not harsh. She requested that her eggs be cooked briefly, not in the pan long at all. I cracked, scrambled, seasoned them, and then put them into the skillet. Those eggs were not in the pan for more than five seconds, and she already yelled in the kitchen to take hers out. I would say, "Grandma, they haven't even been in the pan that long." If I had not taken them out immediately, I kid you not; she would not have eaten those eggs.

We always had something to eat at her house. She allowed me to sleep with her on my first night at her house. It was my first and my last. She told me that I slept horribly and felt as if someone kicked her in the back. Grandma did not allow me to ever sleep with her again. Those days at Grandma's house were memorable. My cousin and I fought once, but other than that, I never got into any trouble there. Those were the days, but now she is resting peacefully in heaven. I will never forget her. Long live, Mutt Dear.

Days at Grandma's house were days I cherished. Not only was it a relaxed environment, but it also gave me peace of mind. I got to get close to a lot of my cousins and aunties. The more I went there, the more mellow I became. My first time going over, I must admit, I was super nervous. I didn't know how they would react or treat me. All that worrying was for nothing; I was welcomed with open arms. Fitting in with the family felt fantastic; I was all smiles. As I visited more, it became easier for me to relax.

The thing I didn't like was Grandma having keloid skin. She told me that she had surgery, and the procedure left her with keloids in her chest area. It spread along the whole chest. When she ate, if any crumbs got inside the keloids, it would itch. She would sometimes use the end of the paper to try to get any crumbs that may have fallen inside the area. I often saw her rub up and down the area quickly when it would itch; I know it was very irritating. I used to feel so sorry for her because I could only imagine how that bothered her daily.

The discomfort with her skin didn't stop her show though. But yeah, this was one of my safe spots. If my dad had been able to raise us alongside my mother, things would have been a little different. Mom did a great job, but it would have been even better. The combination of both parents would have put all the pieces together. If he were around, a lot of things would have been better. I felt that he would've protected us as I imagined he would have.

As a child, losing a parent to death, the streets, drugs, prison, or whatever is hard. The decisions don't only affect the individual, but they have a significant impact on the people who love them. I never resented my dad for his decisions, but it stirred up anger and frustration over the years. There was a lack of support, and the love surrounding me wasn't there. Although in my heart and his that he wanted to be there, he wasn't. We couldn't turn back the hands of time and just endured.

Throughout the years, I became afraid to show emotions. I was scared even to show love because I feared betrayal. Yes, it was scary. I walked around as if I didn't have feelings most of the time, as if I didn't care. Deep inside, I did. *Showing emotions is a form of weakness,* I thought. Eventually, it formed this formidable wall in me. Nothing could hurt me—like, I didn't need anyone—while scared of letting anyone get close to me just to be let down. It was my secret.

The objective was to hurt you before you hurt me. So how did I do that? Once the behavior in you changed, my behavior moved accordingly. I held grudges for a long time. It was difficult for anyone to get close to me, so it was shocking to lower my guard and then be betrayed. The anger was built over the years, so my attitude became horrible. Caring about other people's feelings didn't affect me. I recall my mom telling me that I need to change that. Evil thoughts, negative talk, and bad behavior should not be considered the norm. It just couldn't be.

We can't do anything about what will happen to us in life. We can't stop it or put it on pause. Despite not having my dad, God still made a way for us. He blessed us with some fantastic people in our life. God brought us through the toughest situations. During that time, it was more complex than now.

Every setback we encounter along this journey is only an opportunity in disguise. You will acquire knowledge, become sturdy, and grow. Again, will you allow it to make or break you?

Life is just so not fair. No one understands it. One thing for sure and two things for certain, we live to die. One day, we will all have to leave this world whether we want to or not. We have that birth date and that expiration date called *death*. One of the biggest things I had to learn was to live and not *exist*. Living day-to-day and just existing was very miserable. There were plenty of days when getting out of bed was for me hard. Lying in bed and sleeping helps me not think about many things. How many of you guys have ever felt like that?

Depression is natural and underrated. When someone is going through the motions, don't make it worse. You'll never know how you could be saving a life. Nowadays, people do a lot for shows and likes. If someone is at their lowest or breaking point, help them. Everyone faces their life difficulties, and some hide them better than others. It could be them today, and it could be you tomorrow. Imagine trying to endure all that the world has thrown at you. Tough, right? Yeah, I know the feeling. Coping with a lot of childhood trauma wasn't easy. Then, on top of it, I did not even realize it was a problem until way later in life.

There were times when people around me would be pleased, but my level of happiness couldn't match. It couldn't match because I was miserable. The saying "Misery loves company" is a fact. Not that I didn't want to be happy for others, but I just couldn't. Miserable, angry, unhappy, envious, and living in darkness took complete control over my life. Finding happiness was difficult, and maintaining it was even more challenging. Full of anger from the past and trying to help myself, I didn't succeed. Being envious of others because things didn't go as planned for my life was damaging.

Coping without my dad growing up was just something we had to do. In my younger days, I didn't realize how blessed we were. Dad made a decision that caused us to be affected. Yet instead of looking at the bigger picture, for me, the picture wasn't even there. There are so many children without a dad or who aren't active in their lives. Yeah, he was many miles away, but getting to see him every or every other weekend was still a plus. As children, we want what we want. For example, when a child doesn't get what they want from a store, they cry, hoping the cries and tears will change their parents' mindset.

At least we could still talk to him and didn't have to visit him in the graveyard. We got a chance to hug and love him. Then not to mention, God blessed us with my granddad, who stepped up into our lives. Following that, we had a Mom. My mom was everything.

Of course, other family and friends helped in making life a little better.

Letter to my father:

Dear Dad,

I wanted to write this letter to you to say I love and forgive you. I forgive you for your decisions that might not have been the best. I forgive you for not being there when I needed you the most. It hurt losing you to prison because I had to learn how to live without you during that difficult time. Many days and nights, I cried for you and wanted you to just be there. I wish you had been at my sports events; I would have done even better if you had been there.

Looking around in the crowd, not seeing you or Mom used to hurt. The love you showed us, I needed that. Your love was unconditional, and that is what I love so much about you. There is absolutely nothing that will take that away from you. Thank you for allowing me to come and live with you once you were released. I always knew I wanted to better myself when I was young, and you made that happen for me.

Dad, the past is behind us now, and living in this future has been such a joy. You may have missed a lot, but you did rebuild. We rose again. Dad, you may have put on that brave face, but I knew deep inside you were falling apart. Thank you for loving us and going above and beyond.

Signed,
Your baby girl

CHAPTER 6

Transitioning

High school days were fun, but I still had my moments. If I could do a redo, I would. My days and memories at Shaw High School were good. We represented the class of 2004 well. Since my sister and I were only eleven months apart, we were in the same grade. My sister and I were in the same grade throughout high school, which was difficult. We tend not to get along at school but were decent at home. Crazy, right? However, we always had each other's backs throughout the chaos.

Advancing through our school years created quite the story for us. It was the ride, no matter which grade or how old we were. We encountered the best teachers, coaches, principals, and students who came through our school. No, our high school was not perfect, but it was perfect for us in its own little way. As always, we had to cxpcrience the bad with the good. For me, the good days always outweigh the bad. School was everything and a break from home for me.

Learning was always a priority throughout my days, and I was an honor student but occasionally brought in C's, too. My mom did not have to worry much about boys or getting into significant trouble. Although I experienced a few mishaps in my junior and senior years, they were minor and related to fighting. Since I was a tomboy, boys weren't in my view. I was always a part of the sports team (basketball, softball, tennis, etc.). When one season ends, another one begins. It kept me occupied.

Running track was my least favorite, and softball was my favorite. I never liked running track because I hated running long distances. Tennis was fun as well once we got the hang of it. Sports kept me active even though I was always nervous. My talent for sports was good, and most of the time, my nerves got the best of me. For whatever reason, when I get nervous, I function as if my entire system shuts down. I recalled every time I tried out for sports, I was all over the place. Nevertheless, I would still make the team.

I preferred softball over basketball any day. Softball was my favorite because I was better at it than any other sport. I even received the Rookie of the Year award in my first year of playing. The balls were big and complex, but that was not a concern of mine. I watched others get injured from the balls. Once, my friend was pitching, and she got hit in the face with a ball. From the sound of the contact, you would've thought the ball broke something; however, she was okay. When I first started playing softball, my position was either right or left field. Remember that when I joined the team, I was extremely nervous.

I would miss so many balls batted out in the outfield during practices. I couldn't catch them. It's not that I was afraid of the ball or didn't know how to play, just nervous. See, my nervousness was on another level. It seemed as if I couldn't do anything once those butterflies kicked in. Again, my nerves got the best of me during the first couple of games and practices. After practicing a lot, I got the hang of it and got more in the groove. It helped me to become more relaxed and show my talent.

I received rookie of the year at our sports banquet for my first year. The news surprised me because I didn't think I deserved it. I beat up on myself a lot and hid the truth. The more I played, the more games became easier. Over the years, I started playing second base or shortstop. Our coach, Coach Thomas, was excellent, and she always looked out for us. For example, she would pay for our food or make sure we made it home safely after the games. Sometimes, she would even drive us home. Coach Thomas was my favorite coach, and she knew it.

My best friend, Tawana, played on the same team. Imagine the two peas in the pod on the same team. After practice, we would always walk home together since we lived down the street from each other. During those walks home, we had competitive talks. She would think she was better than me and vice versa. We discussed what mishaps happened during practices. Sometimes, the conversations would go left, but we still brushed it off by the time we reached the end of our streets.

My best friend and I joined forces at an incredibly early age. Second grade was when the friendship began. Tawana, better known as Moon, lived down the street from me, so we were only two minutes away. We talked every single day. When you saw her, you also saw me, and vice versa. They would call us two peas in the pod. She was my true backbone, and the love grew stronger throughout the years. We had our good times and bad times along this journey, but we always found ourselves back like we never left.

Tawana will always have a soft spot in my heart. As I mentioned, it was hard for me to show emotions, but I would for her. There was not anything we would not do for each other. We talked every single day, even if we hung out. You would think our parents would love us since we were so close, but it was the opposite. Tawana lived with her grandma, and she did not care much for me; my mom also disliked her. Strange. We never gave them a reason to even act like that toward us. It never stopped us from being friends, though.

Her grandma did not want me to visit; my mom didn't want her at our house either. It was weird. We never got into trouble. We always questioned their reasonings and never allowed how they felt to break us apart. Sometimes we laughed about it. When Tawana saw my mom or I saw her grandma, we called each other and discussed their behavior. One time, I saw her grandma in the grocery store. She barely spoke. She saw my mom at the gas station once, but she didn't even say hello. So conversations like that would be funny to us.

My best friend was a fighter like me. I witnessed some of her fights, and she did mine. The thing was, we never tried to fight each other. It was like going against our code. However, one day, a family friend got into her head to fight me. They knew we could both fight and wanted to determine the winner, so they placed a bet. We were all playing basketball outside the house, having a wonderful time.

My mom brought my brother's basketball goals, and our neighbor's grandson had one. The neighborhood would tend to gather up there.

We were outside my house when they dared us to fight each other. Fighting my best friend was out of the question. On the other hand, she thought that since they hyped her up, she would beat me up or something. She hit me. This girl struck me in the face, which is when all bets were off. That day, we fought over five rounds. The last round was when we called it quits. By then, I wrapped her shirt around her face and neck. She was yelling, "I cannot breathe." Do you think I cared? Um, *no*. I refused to let go.

That is when the neighbor kids broke us apart and stopped the fight. I could not believe this girl hit me. I was *livid*. I was so mad at her that I did not care if she couldn't breathe; I was ready for another round. The kids kept getting in between us so that we couldn't fight. It took me a minute to calm down. Guess what? Regardless, we still made up that exact day as if nothing happened. We even walked to softball practice the next day, laughing at the fight. Our petty disagreements did not get too severe for us just to cut each other off completely.

There would have been a grudge if this had been anyone else. My love for her would not allow me to be upset with her for a long time. Plus, she would do things that wouldn't allow me to. This friendship meant a lot to me, so for her to allow someone to come in and try to destroy us was weird. It was a prime example of how the devil works. He would utilize individuals to attempt to destroy you, but you must exert all efforts to prevent it. What did fighting prove? It didn't prove anything at all. The whole time we were fighting, they were laughing. In life, never allow others to destroy anything going on in your life. Whether it's marriage, friendship, or whatever, please do not allow others to come in between.

Two peas in a pod—whatever she was down for, you could count me in and vice versa. We made some crazy decisions too—for example, the time when I stole my mother's car. Before taking the vehicle without permission, I used sticks to align the car when repositioning. This way, parking wasn't an issue when I returned the vehicle. On this particular day, my best friend was in the front seat. While joyriding, the vehicle lost control and spun around in the middle of the road. Many cars were heading in our direction. All I did was close my eyes. To this day, an angel was watching over us. We ended up on the side of the road, no accident. Immediately, I drove back home.

It was a scary sight and moment to be in. That incident still did not stop me from stealing the car though. You would think it would. Um, nope. Weeks after this, my mom came home upset. She demanded her car key. See, when she was away, I made another set of keys. Yes, I had my own set of keys. We were getting away with it until Mom received the call. One of her friends saw her car downtown. The friend stated that she was trying to stop her. Mom was puzzled because she knew she wasn't downtown and at work. The friend told her that someone was driving her car, and from there, Mom knew it had to be me. Trying to act like no keys were in my possession was about to cause Mom a case. So eventually, I handed her the key.

Stealing a car in my younger years was not something taken seriously. I did not know the danger of a car while just joyriding. No seat belts while speeding. A lot of people died in a car accident. I thank God we could live to see another day regardless of our unpleasant decisions. Again, this is an example of how a decision could affect you and everyone around you. Everything happened for a reason. Imagine if my mom had not found out about the car when she did.

Sports were activities that my best friend and I participated in. Every softball player that year had to undergo a physical to play sports. During this physical check, we all thought we were getting a shot. I was not too fond of needles. A lot of the players finished theirs and passed, then I went. I passed mine as well. While we were waiting in the lobby waiting area, two players were left to complete their physicals. One of them was my best friend. We were all in the lobby talking, laughing, and enjoying our passing.

Minutes later, we saw my best friend walking back into the lobby with tears in her eyes. There were a lot of tears coming down her face. Immediately, we assumed the doctor did something inappropriate to her. We started asking her questions.

"Did he touch you?"

"What happened?"

We were wondering what was wrong because she was speechless. Coach Thomas was trying to calm her down. That is when we found out she was pregnant. Yes, she was pregnant. My best friend was pregnant. Everyone's faces were shocked. It felt like we were in a dream; this could not be real.

In our teen years, accepting that was not in my thoughts. It was a misunderstanding or a false test or something. It was just shocking. I knew she was dating, but dang. I was a tomboy, so sex wasn't even in the category. If I did have a crush on a guy, my way of telling him was beating up on him or doing crazy stuff. It was my form of showing emotions. Weird. The lobby got extremely quiet immediately. We all were looking around, speechless to the point you could hear a pin drop. Our faces were clueless, heads puzzled, so many thoughts running.

My best friend was only thirteen years old. *How can a thirteen-year-old be pregnant? How is that even possible?* These were my thoughts! I was stressed and worried at the same time. I was stressed because I was her friend and could do nothing. I was worried because I did not know how her grandma or family would take the news. Not to mention, she could not play any more sports with me. We didn't know much about life at this age because we were still living in the moment.

We all left the clinic and went home. Once home, I cried for my best friend. I even tried to call her, but no answer. I did not know what to think. Since I could not reach her, I walked to the end of the street and began to see if I could see her. I felt I would get lucky because I refused to knock at her door now. I waited for a while. Cars passed me, but none of them were her. I was kicking rocks on the way home, just worried about her. My thoughts were all over the place because when she hurt, I hurt.

My best friend was pregnant and only a baby herself. I was stressed out as if it was me; that's how much my love for her was present. Finally, the next day, she called me, and we talked. I felt relieved a little. I could hear the disappointment in her voice as she spoke. Although she was pregnant, we still hung together a little, but not as much. I never judged or questioned her. Only a child herself, I am sure she already felt judged. One thing that I loved throughout her pregnancy was that her family stood alongside her. She never showed the downside to her pregnancy; she was so strong.

During my best friend's last trimester, we had a falling out. Yes, we stopped talking and hanging around each other. Others tried to come in between us to destroy us with lies. At first, it was working, and we stopped talking. One day, I was walking in the gym when she approached me. She asked me if I talked about her. I felt defensive because I had heard she was also talking about me, even though I didn't have an issue with her. Now I wasn't planning on fighting; she was pregnant, for God's sake. While talking, she hit me in the face.

When she hit me, I pushed her back. From last time, I forgot she was pregnant for a second. We got tangled up, and many stepped in to pull us apart. I was so shocked that she hit me *again* like the prior fight at my house. I couldn't do anything about it because she was carrying an innocent baby. I'm not going to lie; I was upset to the max once again. See, we have been down this road before but overcame it. But it wasn't like that this time. I was upset with her for a long time; she was my friend, and trying to fight me was devastating. I didn't want to see or hear from her. When I would see her, I just walked past her, not saying one word.

Weeks after the incident, I discovered she had her baby, and I was happy. I was delighted that she had a safe delivery, but I was still in my feelings about her. We agreed that I would be there, but since that happened, I went to the hospital a day afterward. No matter how I felt, I couldn't be upset with her. This girl was my best friend; we were like sisters. We acted like sisters. We would argue and fight like sisters. That bond was like—you can be mad today, but get it together so we can move forward.

Once my best friend had her baby, things changed. She was more mature than before. Her attitude toward life has shifted; I knew she wanted to be the best mother. Moon was not only athletic, but she was charming. She had beautiful, incredibly soft baby hair. I recall braiding it multiple times; it would easily slide through the comb. Those memories were everything. Her baby was like my god-baby, and I cared for her too. My best friend was a prime example of not giving up. When life throws you those lemons, it's time to make lemonade; that is what she did.

Friends who have your back are scarce. It's best to keep them by your side if you come across them. The word *friend* isn't something that you should take lightly. Not everyone is your friend, and not all have your best interests at heart. Throughout this journey, this was an extensive learning experience for me. Everyone who calls you a friend should not only say it but also show it. There's no one-sided relationship when it comes to a friend. Also, remember that friend(s) come and go, and that's okay. Sometimes, it's necessary to let go of a friendship that no longer serves a purpose; it's okay to move forward without holding grudges.

Letter to my best friend

Dear best friend,

I am incredibly proud of you. You never let anything stop you from moving forward in life. Although you had a child at a young age, you still strived for perfection. I could only imagine what you went through while being a child your-self—all those pregnancy days from all the doctor appointments, being judged by others, still try-ing to attend high school, and so on.

Life is not fair, but you made the best of it. You conquered it, my love. I am happy to call you a true friend, my best friend. You have been by my side since day 1, and I admire you for that. We had some ups and downs, but after all these years, we remained friends. That is all part of a friendship; you will have disagreements, but as true friends, you work through them as we did. Everything was not so peachy.

There were days you got on my nerve and vice versa. The love we have for each other will always be something I cherish for the rest of my life. Thank you for being my friend and sticking by my side. Even though your grandmother didn't care for me and the same for my mom with you, we made it happen. Words couldn't express how proud I am; you are just amazing. You will always have a special place in my heart. I love you, best friend.

Sincerely,
Your best friend

*****

Aside from Tawana, I had other friends, such as Kam, Kenyatta, and Nay, but she and I were much closer. Visiting and hanging out with my other friends, I did enjoy them too. I remember visiting Kam and Nay at their houses a lot too. Since my mom never wanted company at our house, we'd hang out at their house instead. Their parents had no issues with me and welcomed me when I visited. Those were some good old days. Childhood friends are the absolute best. It was all the memories we accumulated over the years. Those memories will never die.

Kam and I were close friends, but sometimes we occasionally disagreed during basketball practices. Her mom and sister were always the sweetest. There were times while visiting when she would argue with her sister, and it would be so funny. Nay and I had a great bond; we never argued and always laughed together. During our high school days, she always drove her parents' vehicles to school or practice, which was fantastic. She started driving young, and I would be right on the passenger side. Kenyatta and I built a friendship and had great memories. Kenyatta and my best friend were always at odds with each other. So, of course, that made it awkward for me.

During our high school years, we embraced dynamic and vibrant lives. As teenagers, we were careless of the world and living our best lives. I wasn't afraid of the world; I just lived in it like a teenager. Since we didn't have a middle school in our small town, once you finished seventh grade, high school was where you transferred to. The teachers will organize a graduation party or ceremony for students at the end of elementary school. Your parents would be there and all the prior teachers; it was lovely. I don't know if a middle school would have made a difference, but to experience one would have been excellent. Since our town was not so big, there would need to be more students to fill the school.

My sister and I were in the first year of high school; we could finally attend school with my brothers. Brothers 1 and 2 were seniors; brother 3 was a sophomore. We only saw each other a little because each grade would go to lunch at a different time, plus the senior classrooms were on the opposite side of the school. There were rare occasions when a lower class took classes with the upper class. For example, driver ed had a mixture of grades when I attended. Other than that, you would take classes with your grade. Therefore, we would see each other after school so we could walk home together.

Going to school with my brothers, my sister and I felt protected. I recalled a time a guy slapped my sister in ISS. ISS was in school suspension, which allowed students to be at school while having a disciplinary action. For instance, it is an excellent reason to go if you are acting up in class. Instead of them suspending you or calling your parents, you would go there to do your work and finish the day. It is just an isolation from the rest of the school. The trailer was outside of the tennis court by the school, so you only had a little to walk. Any who, while in ISS, my sister and this guy argued, and he slapped my sister.

My sister immediately told Brother 2. After school, Brother 2 went looking for the guy who slapped her. They got into a massive fight in the gym, one of the biggest fights ever. While Brother 2 and the guy fought, Brother 3 was struck off guard by the guy's best friend. He struck my brother, and I heard it. Brother 3 immediately started fighting the guy's best friend. Brother 3 wasn't going to fight;

he was just present to ensure no one jumped Brother 2. Not expecting to be hit, this caused rage. Brother 3 was so upset that no one could control him. Our coach was trying to break up the fight, and he started trying to fight him. Coach D wasn't having it. Although he was a teacher and coach on duty, disrespect was something he didn't ride with.

Eventually, the fight was under control. My brothers, the guy, and his best friend got suspended from school for nine days. My mom wasn't upset after she found out what happened. One thing about my mom, she didn't promote fighting, but she never wanted others to harm her kids or bully us. She always told us not to start a fight but to protect ourselves if we ever had to fight. Of all the whipping we received, we never got any for fighting. Something about fighting didn't bother her much.

If I got suspended for something silly, she probably wouldn't have taken it so lightly. For instance, my only suspension was due to fighting. My friend and I fought at school; I got suspended, and she wasn't satisfied. Okay, what happened was a messy girl in the neighborhood lied to her as if we were talking about her. The lies told to her caused her to become upset with me without my knowledge. Not knowing it was an issue between her and me, I only found out at school. Students asked me what was going on between us. I was puzzled, very shocked, and clueless about this. Apparently, in the classroom, she planned a fight without me. Not knowing if this information was accurate, it was brushed off, like whatever attitude.

Then my cousin came into the gym and related information regarding how she planned to fight me and how vigorously she spoke of my name. *BAM,* that was all the information I needed. It must be valid since everyone else was coming to me about this. Immediately, my body jumped up from where I was sitting and ran out of the gym, running directly to the room she was in. Other students, including my sister, ran out of the gym with me. Our high school had three floors; we rarely used the third floor. I ran up the second level through the bathroom and main hallways. Bell rang. My whole intent was to catch the bell before she left the classroom.

When the bell rang, I was only seconds away from the classroom. Upon finally reaching the destination, the students began walking out. I stood by the door waiting. At this point, there were no holds bar. Hearing her voice but not seeing her made me impatient. She finally walked toward the door to leave the classroom. Once I spotted her, I asked her, "What is all that BS you've been talking about me or how you are going to beat me up after school?" Before she could answer the question, I hit her in the face. We began scuffling; she was pulling my hair. I had microbraids; she pulled a few of them out. Teachers and other students broke it up, and she and I were sent to the principal's office.

In the principal's office, I was still upset. What made it worse was that he suspended me and not her. She began crying because she felt as though she didn't hit me and didn't deserve a punishment. How fair was that? She pulled my hair and tried to fight back. Both parties would get suspended back then, whether you won or lost. Moving along, Mom came to the school after the fight to pick me up. No, I didn't get into trouble, but she did fuss. She knew we were friends, so we rode to Cleveland together after the fight. During that ride, we didn't even talk to each other; yes, it was awkward. We were able to overcome that hump; she will always be a friend for life. A brilliant person with a heart of gold; this I experienced firsthand.

This suspension was the only one I experienced throughout my school days. I shouldn't have let other people's words affect my emotions. Listening to others in my ears caused a reaction in me. It was also a lesson for me, sitting at home suspended from school while those who related the information to me were still at school. Trouble is something I rarely get into, especially at school. During my fighting days, it was usually not at school. My last fight was when I got into it with a girl who cut me in the face. Riding in an ambulance to the hospital was not a good feeling. Fighting was ideal for many years because my skills were on point. This fight changed everything.

It happened when I visited my aunt, who lived in the old project, during a BBQ. Believe it or not, this fight wasn't mine. After the BBQ, my sister and I walked across the street to my cousin's house, my aunt's daughter. This girl had beef with my sister and called her the B word. From there, my sister was ready to fight. Remind you, we had food in our hands; laying the food on a random person's trunk was insane. The food could wait. My motive was to de-escalate the situation without beefing with her.

While pulling them apart, the girl yelled, "B, you can get the same thing your sister will get."

"First off, who are you calling a B?" I replied.

She said, "You."

I immediately punched her in the face. From there, she was an enemy. While fighting her, one of her friends hit me in the back of the head along with a grown man. The grown man I did not know, but the girl I did. It was hard to break away from everyone to get to her. They would not let me go for anything, which got me more upset. We were finally pulled apart and taken inside the house. I didn't realize she had cut my face until I saw the blood dripping on my shirt after my cousin mentioned it. Looking down at my white tee full of blood scared me. Everyone was like you may have to go to the hospital; the bleeding would not stop.

Going to the hospital was like a blur. Enjoying the excitement that this girl got beat up by me was life. To me, she never needed to include me in this. Everyone was talking about how badly I beat her up; this blew my head up. When did she even have the time to grab a knife? We all were puzzled. When she was hit by me, from there, she never got the opportunity to fight back. However, witnesses around her said she must have had it on her already, or someone else had given it to her. Still, to this day, this was a mystery.

The white T-shirt and ice were both applied to my face. Shortly, my family started calling us. My mom arrived first. Mom came to the project in a rage and was ready to fight. My brothers were trying to keep her under control. It was the blood she saw that triggered her. She popped the trunk of her car and grabbed a crowbar while calling our cousin Timbo, relating about the guy who hit me. A lot of my family came out that night. That night was wild. It was supposed to be my sister's fight, so why was I in the back of an ambulance?

Walking to the ambulance made it a reality for me. In all honesty, it was at that moment my body shut down. I was very scared.

Ten minutes prior, they saw me jumping around doing this and that. Now having to get in the back of an ambulance was embarrassing. All this drama was never big enough for this. It wasn't the best decision. Entertaining drama and nonsense placed me here. After having time to think inside the ambulance, tears began to roll down my face. Hearing stories of others getting killed in fights or seriously injured was all my mind could think of.

We arrived at the hospital; the doctor told me that I needed stitches. The way my face was bleeding, I was anticipating having a massive cut. Unfortunately, I received seven stitches in my face. The doctor said it was so much blood due to the adrenaline rush. Once released, we headed back home. That night, we received numerous phone calls. The lies had started. One lie was that the girl cut me so severely that they didn't think I would make it. Another one was she cut my throat. We heard it all. The stitches and cuts were tiny; you could barely see it on my face.

The next day, walking to the post office was crazy. People were passing me in their cars, about to run off the road, trying to stare at me. Not to mention, several cars passed me more than one time. Instead of stopping and asking, they drove by slowly to see my face. Again, the cut was minor. After this fight, my eyes were wide awake. My promise was not to get involved in someone else's conflict, regardless of who they are. I thank God that he spared my life; it could have been much worse. From then on, no more fights for me. That was it. At first, my mind wanted revenge. The scar on my face for life is the same as she would get. My heart let it go.

This scar permanently reminds me daily of that mistake I made. As I mentioned earlier in this book, we all make mistakes. Some we can come back from, and others we can't. Living to see another day was my testimony. My story could have ended differently, but God's grace and mercy protected me. Only God knows how reversing time would help me make better choices, but my foot was still in motion since I could not. You never know what to expect, so you should try to live your best life. Life is what it is. You can make some choices but try to make the right ones, especially those that would be beneficial.

Throughout high school, braiding hair was one way to make money. When I first started, charging $50 for some microbraids was very cheap. In a small town, prices for braids were less expensive than if you went to the city or the Africans. In the beginning, the money seemed like a lot. I obtained a lot and got the things I wanted. It helped pay my way throughout high school. Braiding my sister's hair turned into braiding my friends, friends of friends, friends of the family, and by word of mouth, it grew from there. Every week, I had appointments. The only downfall of braiding was the time while standing up. Since micro braids were so small, it took some time to do. I took my time since my work meant a lot to me.

Braiding only one head a day was all for that day. I could not book several clients in one day; my body would not allow me to handle that. During these times, there were good and bad days. Some days, my body would want to lie in bed. Some days, my body will be up and ready. This side hustle was a great idea. My mom didn't have to buy much for me once I began braiding hair. That was cool. I recalled getting my first cell phone, shoes, clothes, little things for school, money for snacks, etc. I thank God for blessing me with a gift to help me and my family. It may be small to others but significant to me. It is good to have your own money; you can spend it however you want.

As the years passed, I maneuvered throughout my freshman, sophomore, and junior years. We were finally *seniors*. Once you hit twelfth grade, you know you don't have long left in school. All those other years flew by so fast, but the taste of a senior was good. *Finally*, as graduation approached slowly, my mind had not decided what next step to take. College was an option. Then moving away from my small town was another option. There were so many dreams I wanted to accomplish. As the senior year continued to move along, the nervousness kicked in. The idea of making everyone proud of me was the golden key. Praying and not worrying were my best options.

Being a part of the class of 2004 had its good and bad times. We were the class that could not get it right to save our souls. It took a lot of work for us to agree on anything, let alone a plan. Planning anything was like a complete waste of time. We did not even go on a senior trip. Yes, no senior trip. Every class each year went on a trip except us. I wonder why we could not make things happen like the other classes. There were supportive sponsors, but it was just our class in general. Although we had our mishaps, the class of 2004 still rocks. We had our good times along the way.

I decided to run for Ms. Shaw High School during my senior year. It has been my dream since elementary school, and I don't know why. My nerves took over as a junior, so I did not run, although I should have. However, I decided to run my last year since I wouldn't get the opportunity again. I was a senior, and there was no turning back. To my surprise, only expecting one or two others to run against me was not the case. A total of four candidates ran. One of the candidates' moms just passed away before this. It was such a sad occasion because she was so sweet and caring. I can only imagine what a tough time they were experiencing.

Finally, the day came. I was super nervous; Brother 1 was my escort. The candidate I hoped for won Ms. Shaw High School, although it wasn't me. One of the teachers told me I came in second place. In a way, I was hoping to win, but if I did not, I really wanted her to. But only God knows best. Sadness was far from how I felt then; I felt more relieved. The weeks leading up to the announcement were stressful. Many thought one of the teachers would cheat since we were so close. There was much talk about that.

One of my teachers and I were extremely close. She was the one teacher who took time with me. She would allow me to visit her big house and go home with her after school if we had a game. She had three sons and no daughters. I would ride to the games with her and get in free every time. Many school kids did not like her, but she was okay with me. Believe it or not, underneath that tough exterior, her heart was pure, and her student's behavior mirrored hers. The reason was that she was different outside school. She and I built a strong bond for sure. Acting up in her class was something you could not get me to do.

Winning Ms. Shaw High School was a big deal for me since my first year, but all that changed. I'm not going to lie; when we arrived home, I cried. I was emotional. I waited for this moment, for it not to play out as I anticipated. It was just mixed emotions. Tears. In life, there will be times you win, and times you will lose. You will not win them all, and you won't lose them all either. That was a time when winning wasn't meant for me. It was a competition. Feeling shamed and disappointed is normal. However, with a competitor, someone will win and lose. It was no way around it. It's not the end of the world. Holding my head up afterward was hard, but I had to do it.

All those memories built over time with Shaw High School; it was finally our time. *Yes*, graduation. It felt as though it was a dream. I never expected time to roll around so fast. Not to mention, my sister and I were graduating the same year. All the schoolwork, walking those hallways, eating the cafeteria food, being in the gym, the teacher getting on your last nerves, switching classes, all the homework, and so on; the time was here—no more high school for us. On the day of graduation, I was so nervous. *Wow*, we are finally here. Graduating with honors meant a lot to me, and finishing was a huge accomplishment—the class of 2004.

There were good and bad. Shaw High School would always be the best. We learned, grew, built, and enjoyed the moment until it was time to say farewell. Thinking back over everything, one thing that didn't prepare me for the real world after high school or even college was the importance of credit. Credit was not a huge factor to me. Not knowing the importance of credit was one thing life taught me the hard way. Having to rebuild my credit score from the low 500s was stressful.

Also, parents should help educate their kids about the importance of credit. Some parents destroy their kids' credit before they are even grown. Yes, it's true. For instance, parents would get bills in their kids' names and allow the bill to get behind. Parents refuse to pay it; now, the innocent child is stuck with debt that they are unaware of, let alone too young to have. I recalled my mom putting the phone bill in my name. One day, I was at my aunt Fluffie's house when my mom called. My name came across the caller's ID. Looking crazy, I thought, *Why is the phone bill in my name?* I questioned Mom about that. The good thing is that she always paid her bills, so debt was not really an issue.

Public communication is another form of material that I recommend being taught more in high school now. Growing up, speaking the country talk was natural to me. Surrounded by others who talk like me, you could not tell the difference in the language barrier. I'm not saying that the way I spoke was incorrect, but the delivery needed to be up to par. For example, words such as *shrimp* and *street* gave off the *k* sound. My vocabulary could have been more pleasant. Once I moved to the big city, my grammar was just divergent. Learning to speak was challenging. Later in this book, you will understand what I mean. Being able to speak effectively is essential. Believe it or not, you will face challenges throughout this journey.

Adulthood

After graduating from high school, I needed to clarify my life plans. See, at first, my dad was planning to attend our graduation. All those years, he was now free. Somehow, that plan did not fall through. He was reassigned to a halfway house in Georgia and eventually moved with his wife after being released. Even though he missed our graduation, he intended to make it up to us. Graduation was in May 2004; my sisters and I went to Georgia in July 2004. My sisters returned home in August, but I stayed. Planning my future in Georgia would be advantageous, giving me more opportunities.

Immediately, college searches were on the agenda. Searching for different colleges was stressful. Since I haven't resided in Georgia for a year, the out-of-state fees were insane. Eager to avoid the delay, I took the initiative to select a college to attend. Student loans and grants were my glide through school. My mom co-signed for the student loans, which made things much better. Student loans were insane, not to mention the interests built over time. I wished I would have just paid my way instead of taking out the student loans. That was a debt that lingered for years after graduation.

Since the college was in the Buckhead area, far from home, the bus was my form of transportation. Dad was working nights, and my stepmom was working during the days. They only had one vehicle at the time. Plus, the bus was cheaper, although it took forever to get there and back home. It was $2.50 going and coming. Usually, the pass was what I purchase for the week since it was cheaper and more convenient. The ride home was always about one hour and a half every single day. My constant prayer was, "Please do not let the bus break down. It will take longer." My day would start at 5:00 every morning to ensure I caught the bus by 6:00 a.m.

Dad would drive me to the bus stop most of the time. He would be getting off work around that time anyway, so it was not an issue. About three months later, Brother 1 moved here with us. He stayed with my dad until he could get his first apartment. The company he worked for was going out of business in Mississippi, so he just transferred to Georgia. It was fascinating for me. Not only was he staying with Dad, but he was riding the same bus with me every day. It made the bus ride more relaxed. We would separate at the train station once we reached a certain point.

While enrolled in school, I needed money. So, I started putting in job applications. Only two companies called me for an interview for months out of all the applications I filled out. I was losing my patience and getting discouraged while being homesick. It was all kicking in at once. Less than two weeks later, my uncle Andrew moved to Georgia. We all lived with Dad, but I had my own room. My uncle was only in Georgia for about a week and landed a job.

On the other hand, I was applying like crazy and couldn't even get a job. *What did my uncle do more than me?* He started working at Ryan's Steakhouse as a cook. Here I was still applying for other jobs. My uncle Andrew informed me that Ryan's was hiring. The next day, my dad took me up there to apply. Less than a week later, the manager called me back.

Words could not express the feeling of excitement. Making $9.50 an hour seemed like good money; it was my only income. Starting as a cashier, a veteran cashier challenged all the newbies. Since she had been there a while, she would have the new cashiers do her job. I did her work and mine; however, I caught on to what she was doing once I understood my job duties and the flow. It was my first job, so the working industry was new.

Brother 1 only lived with my dad briefly. Then, he got his apartment. Boy, was I happy. I moved in with him eventually. It was so much more convenient, not to mention it was in a nice area near downtown. The apartment was near my school, and it took me only a short time to travel back and forth. During the first few months after relocating to Georgia, my enthusiasm for school was at its highest, and I rated it 10 out of 10. I wanted to be the first of my siblings to attend and complete college. My siblings had intentions to move forward, but life reversed. So to hold my end of the family, I was determined. The first college was adventurous.

I was this country girl in the big city that had to adjust. My first day of college in the fall of 2004 was bittersweet. Although my nerves kicked in, I managed to get through the day. I met my best friend, Dunta'. I entered the college campus on my first day, and he was excited. I spoke, and then he spoke while still heading in different directions. Heading to the counselor's office to finalize my schedule was my focus. Lo and behold, my first class, there he goes again. I never would have thought we would build such a fantastic bond.

Being in the same class as Dunta' made me feel comfortable. After a while, we all built friendships. College was so fun but different. My favorite professors were Dr. Whitest and Mr. Laurent. Dr. Whitest was a true warrior when it came to ensuring that her students completed assignments. She and I continued the professional relationship after I left. Mr. Laurent was from the islands, and his accent was everything. One of my friends had a crush on him. All she would do was discuss this man in class and blush. He was a nice-looking guy, but he wasn't someone I had a crush on like her; I was strictly professional with him. His class was enjoyable.

Mr. Laurent had us write a biography paper about ourselves. I wasn't expecting him to have us read it in front of the class. When it was my turn to read my paper, I was so embarrassed. My paper was written exactly how I talked. It contained many slang words along with the slang ghetto talk. While standing in the front reading my paper, the whole class laughed, including him. During some parts of reading, he would stop me and ask me questions about my slang words. My grammar could have been better. It didn't bother me at the time, so I laughed along. If I could replay my presentation, you would think that a third grader might have written my paper.

When you learn better, you do better. After taking more classes, my English improved. I had to come to terms with the fact that I couldn't speak the way I used to. It's all fun and games around friends, but speaking in front of others isn't. After completing a few semesters, college started to get dull. My energy level for college was different. I started missing classes, and now I must catch up on my work. The main reason for my decision was my exhaustion from the lengthy bus commutes to and from school. It was okay initially, but I wasn't feeling it during those cold months. My mom then decided to give me one of her vehicles.

It was a great relief to be able to drive to school. I did not have to be on the bus or train with the craziness. You never know what you will see daily while using public transportation, standing in the cold waiting for the train or bus. But being able to just jump in my car and ride out with the heater blasting was a plus. While driving, seeing others waiting for the bus made me appreciate my blessings. Just jumping in your vehicle to get from place to place was the best. I appreciate my mom for blessing me the way she did.

In July 2005, I met Duke. Duke is the father of my children but was my boyfriend at the time. While living with my brother, one day I passed him and his brother a few times in the apartments on Spruce Street where we lived. However, my neighbors rarely saw me or knew my name. This summer, my best friend, Moon came to visit. One day, she was outside talking to him and his brother on the stairs; I walked right past. She entered the house and told me he wanted to speak to me. Remind you, I saw him a few times, but not so close. I went outside, and we began talking. He was not my type because he was so slim. After learning about his personality, I realized that he was so sweet.

We began to hang out a lot and build our bond. After a few months of dating, I became pregnant with my first child. I was shocked, along with others. "Sharoslyn with a baby" was what I heard for a long time. Again, I was a tomboy, so I wasn't too serious about dating. I fought with every boyfriend I dated. My relationship did not last too long because of that. But after going to the doctor, it was confirmed. After finding out I was pregnant, I began to get sick. I was so sickly to the point that my saliva made me vomit. It was so severe that my health began to deteriorate quickly. My weight decreased dramatically; I could not hold any food down, was very weak, and could barely talk and walk. All I wanted to do was lay in bed all day.

Brother 1 would bring me food home when he got off work, but I could not eat it. It would sit in the room until he came to clean it. Brother 1 did not realize how severely ill I became until one day; I went to the emergency room. While lying in bed, Duke's mother came to visit me. She said she wanted to check on me since she hadn't seen me for a while. When she opened my room door, she began crying uncontrollably. When she saw me, she immediately wanted to take me to the hospital. Somehow, they got me out of bed and in the car. I couldn't walk; my legs were so weak. Since this was my first pregnancy, I did not know how hard it would affect my body. To this day, I feel that his mother saved my life.

Once we arrived at the hospital for the first time, my potassium, iron, and all were so low. They gave me plenty of fluids and then released me. The minute they released me, I felt okay until I returned home. It felt like I vomited all those fluids back up. So I was back at the hospital the next day. The hospital kept me this time because my condition was quite serious. I went from being 146 pounds to 99 pounds. I was in the hospital for two weeks. While in the hospital, Duke found a job to save money for the baby. He would visit me at the hospital when he could. One time, my love got me a stuffed bear and balloons. Again, he was so sweet.

After being released from the hospital, I knew I would need help. My mother came to pick me up to go back to Mississippi so she could help me. My sister rode with her; she had just had her baby but came anyway. I didn't want to leave then, but this was the best decision. It gave Duke time to work without having to look after me or stress. I moved back home during my pregnancy, but we communicated daily. Duke and his family came down for my baby shower. He was emotional during this visit because he missed me and vice versa. I was more focused on getting myself together and getting back healthy.

On June 13, 2006, my baby girl was born. Since Duke had to travel by bus to Mississippi, he missed the birth of my daughter, but he made it later that night. He was so excited. We both were young and began parenting at such a young age. We never got to know each other. We went straight into parenting mode. After two months, I moved back to Georgia to be with my family. I was grateful that he held it down while I was away and to ensure that we were straight when we returned. He worked extremely hard and got a truck while saving money. God blessed me with a great person who wanted to be a part of their child's life.

When I had my daughter, I did not know how to love her because I didn't even know how to love myself. I knew I loved her because this was my child, but I didn't know how to express it if that made sense. I would stare at her and pray that I would make all the right decisions and break any generational curse. It took me a minute for everything to kick in and become transparent. It was real; I was a mother. I could not believe that I had a whole child. Parenting did not come with instructions, but we did our best. Upon relocating to Georgia, we temporarily resided with Duke's sister. I appreciate her hospitality during our transitional period. However, I opted to relocate back to Brother 1 due to certain unresolved matters.

He lived in a one-bedroom apartment since moving from his previous residence. My daughter and I would sleep on the couch in the living room. We were saving money to get our apartment, so I was okay with the fact that we wouldn't be there for long. Everything was going well until Brother 2 came over one day. Brother 2 could not do anything suitable to save his life. I love him dearly, but the truth is the truth. He couldn't hold a job for long and often lived with others. My mother took care of his kids and so on. Although he couldn't keep a job, he always had new shoes and clothes. The women he dated would buy these things. I always hoped he would pull himself together and do the right thing one day.

Brother 1 didn't want Brother 2 to come over, which I understood. It was his apartment; Brother 2 should have respected that. However, he didn't directly tell Brother 2; he wanted me to relay the message to him. The next day, Brother 2 came over, and I politely passed on the message, convincing Brother 1 to talk to him directly. At first, I thought everything was fine after Brother 1 shared his feelings. But after Brother 2 and his friend left, Brother 1 called a meeting. Less than a week after that, I decided to move out.

Living with my brother was great, but I felt it was time to find my place. I made sure to contribute by paying rent and helping out, but I knew it was best for me to move on. Before leaving, I wrote a heartfelt letter to my brother to express my gratitude and emotions. Unlike my other siblings, I've always felt a strong bond with Brother 1. After returning his key and packing my things, I left for a hotel for a few nights while figuring out my apartment situation. Despite the uncertainty, I was determined to find an apartment as soon as possible, so I took a leap of faith and started looking immediately instead of waiting on Duke.

I drove to the apartments, completed my application, and paid the $50 application fee. The lady informed me that it could take about a week or so to get an update on my application status. I was okay with it since I had enough money to stay at a hotel for about a week. During this time, Brother 2 ensured I was okay and stayed at the hotel with us. Duke wanted me to return to his sister's house, but I was closer to my job on that side of town, so I preferred staying at the hotel until further notice. Duke would come by daily but stay with his sisters since his job was closer.

After three long days of waiting for an update, I called the apartments, but they still had no update for me. I gave up hope and started planning to move back home. I prayed and asked God for a sign to help me decide whether to stay in Georgia. The next day, the apartments called and said my application was approved. However, I still faced a dilemma because I needed $729 to move in and get my keys. Although we had the $729, I didn't consider the cost of furniture and other necessities. My thoughts were moving faster than my pockets.

God made a way for us to get our first apartment finally. I was more than joyful. It was different having your own place. You can do whatever you like without rules from others. We went out and bought new furniture and everything we needed. Over time, we collected more things. As young parents, we pulled it off with God's help. Everything happened for a reason. What the devil meant for the bad, God reversed it for the good.

We were young and doing the best we could. But once we moved in together, the arguments started. Duke would always let me win, even when I was wrong. We'd argue over the most minor things. Looking back, I wonder how often I kicked him out and tossed his clothes outside. I was immature, and our arguments would escalate, involving our families. His family and I had plenty of arguments, and I was often blunt with my choice of words, regretting them later. Once said, words cannot be unsaid, and some of my actions were not right.

But Duke understood me like no one else, so I felt closer to him. He is the most patient person I know and always went above and beyond for his family. I am grateful, even though I struggle to express it. Duke had his faults too, but God knew what he was doing when he brought us together. Moving to Georgia changed my life, and Duke's ambition immensely helped me.

Letter to my love

Dear My Love,

I want to express my gratitude for loving me even when I couldn't love myself. Thank you for always being there for me, even when things were tough. Your love for me is beyond words, and I am truly grateful. You always go above and beyond for me and your family. You bring light into my life, even during the darkest of days. You are my king, and I am forever your queen.

We've had our share of arguments and fights throughout our relationship. Against all odds, we've reached this point, and I couldn't be more pleased.. As we've grown older, we've also grown more mature. We can't change the past but can move forward from it. Despite all the hardships that we've faced, you've always found your way back to me.

Sometimes, I didn't always show my love or appreciation for you, but that doesn't mean that I didn't love you. I truly believe that God brought us together for a reason. He knew exactly what he was doing when our paths crossed. You have enriched my life, and I am grateful for all you do. Thank you for being a fantastic father to our children. You consistently go the extra mile, embodying true royalty in every sense of the word. Losing your father at a young age was difficult, and you struggled for a while. But you were determined to make something of yourself and did just that. I have watched you grow and transform into a fantastic person over the years.

Keep striving for perfection, my love, because God will see us through it all. Thank you for always being there for me, supporting me, and caring for me. You are my true friend, lover, protector, and provider. No matter where this journey takes us, please know I will always love you.

Yours truly,
Your wife

*****

After having my daughter, I put school on hold. The drive for school wasn't there, and I focused on my child and work. However, I was determined to go back to school and graduate. I became complacent with my job(s) and went off course from my vision. But then, out of nowhere, colleges started sending letters to the house. At first, I threw them in the trash, but then I realized that college had become more flexible. If I could work and go to school simultaneously, that would be a plus for me. So I did some research and contacted the school.

In 2009, after a two-and-a-half-year break, I returned to school, but this time, I transferred to a different college, a virtual school that was more convenient for me. Although I occasionally visited the campus, most of my classes were virtual. Virtual courses are often seen as easy, but my experience proved otherwise. The main challenge was consistency and dedication. Some days, I did not feel like completing my homework, but I had to push myself. After a few months, I realized I was struggling and decided to drop a few classes to get myself together. Once I felt ready, I resumed my studies and was determined to finish.

In 2012, I graduated with an associate degree in criminal justice, a significant achievement. I was the first person in my family to go to college, let alone graduate. I intended to work in law enforcement, but after a few jobs in the field, I realized I wanted to pursue a career in the corporate world, specifically in human resources. So in 2013, I enrolled again, majoring in business administration for my bachelor's degree.

Throughout my employment, I worked for some great companies. I also met some great people from each job and built a lot of relationships over the years.

These experiences were excellent, and I learned a lot. I worked as a cabin service worker at the airport for six months. I needed more money at the time, so I resigned after six months. From there, I began working as a contractor at the front desk at the Twin Towers. There, I had the opportunity to meet and take pictures with the governor, commissioners, and others. One person who significantly influenced me was Ms. Bankston, who worked with me at the front desk. She was like a second mom to me.

Contracting with Google as a console operator was my favorite job. It had a relaxed and fun environment with a campus café, free meals, colorful walls, and scooters. I met my close friends April and Ramone, and later Heath. All employees were friendly, and the campus was off-limits to unauthorized people. After a massive layoff, I was reassigned to a different site and left the company. I then worked part-time at the aquarium, enjoying my flexible schedule, fun and outgoing manager, and colleagues Bianca, Adam, and Tameka.

After three years, I decided to start saving for my first home and needed more money. I applied for a position at Turner and got hired after an interview. During training, I was concerned about being assigned to the second shift, which would affect my child and school. I spoke with the Vice President, Sam, who said he would attempt to see what he could do since the schedule was already out. I started my on-the-job training on the second shift and had to wait for a decision regarding the first shift.

The first few days passed, and I still hadn't received any updates about my requested schedule, making the nights increasingly challenging. My mind was preoccupied with my daughter, and I decided that I would quit my job if I didn't hear anything by the following night. I prayed and asked God for a sign. The next day, my supervisor told me I would be on the first shift. My soul was full of excitement.

However, I still had to finish the remaining week on the second shift. I was still happy after hearing the news, though.

I completed the rest of the on-the-job training the following week during the first shift. To this day, I am grateful to God for touching Sam's heart and helping me. He will always have a special place in my heart for the blessing.

In 2015, while working at Turner, I graduated and achieved my dream of earning another degree. However, I became distracted by my current job and lost sight of my aspirations in the human resources field. I had grown comfortable in that role and failed to pursue opportunities for advancement. Instead, I focused on investing in my current area of work. Over the next two years, I received two promotions. Looking back, I realize that putting my dreams on pause was a wrong decision, and I'll explain why later.

This job was an excellent opportunity for my personal and professional growth. The work environment was mainly male-dominated and had high expectations. I worked for Turner and had the chance to interact with news anchors, take a full tour of the building, and more. It was all new to me, but I cherished every moment. I enjoyed working with amazing people such as Michelle, Lenny, Larry, Misti, JB, Mike, Mama Rogers, and more; I formed many close relationships with my colleagues. One person I became particularly close with was Lenny. Although we weren't initially close, we developed a strong bond over time. Despite forming other relationships, this one was extraordinary.

Our relationship had grown so much that we talked almost daily, even outside work. Lenny knew my family, and I knew his. We were good friends. One week at work, I noticed that Lenny's energy seemed off, but I didn't think much of it because everyone went through tough times. Later that week, we talked on the phone, and out of nowhere, he asked me how I would feel if he were no longer here. I ignored the question the first time. The question took me aback, but I answered it after being asked twice. I replied, "I would be sad," and asked him why he was asking that.

I needed clarification but didn't put a lot of energy into it and continued our conversation. In the middle of the conversation, he received a knock at the door. Immediately, he abruptly ended the call. It was strange, and I didn't think much of it. After hours passed, I heard nothing. So before I went to bed, I tried to call back. No answer. Again, I didn't think anything of it because we would see each other at work the next day. I was wrong. I woke up to a "goodbye" text message.

My heart sank as I read the text message. It was already 5:00 in the morning, and I had received this message from my friend the previous night. I immediately called, but there was no answer. I tried to shake off the feeling that something wasn't right, but I couldn't focus on anything else. I couldn't even get ready for work because my mind was racing with thoughts. I was trying to figure out what *goodbye* meant in the message. Maybe my friend had decided to resign from work?

Finally, I managed to calm myself, got ready for work, and headed out. However, I couldn't shake off the feeling that something was wrong. I kept calling my friend's phone, but there was still no answer.

My friend might have arrived early at work, so I expected to see his car in the parking deck. But to my surprise, my friend's car wasn't there. I remained optimistic, thinking my friend might have swapped shifts with someone else.

When I arrived, I asked a coworker if they had heard from my friend. The coworker received the same text message as me. We could not figure out what was going on. I tried calling my friend again during my break, but there was still no answer. At that moment, I knew something was wrong. I spoke to my manager; she asked if anything was unusual during my last conversation with my friend. It struck me that something terrible happened to my friend.

From there, I was informed that his sister called because he was on suicide watch. Later, I discovered that's who knocked at the door while we were on the phone. Management decided to send an officer to the location for a courtesy check. My heart was beating so fast because I was in disbelief. There is no way something happened when we were just on the phone the day prior. It was less than twenty-four hours to be exact, so it just couldn't be that bad.

So I didn't hear anything else the rest of the day. When it was time to clock out, they called an emergency briefing. With that, I knew my friend was no longer with us. I felt something terrible had happened, and reality finally kicked in no matter how hard I tried not to allow it to. I refused to go to the briefing; I just couldn't. It was during the briefing that they announced his passing. My heart was broken, and I was speechless with that blank stare.

Coworkers began crying, and everyone was in total shock. My heart felt like it had fallen to the floor, and someone stepped over it. I was speechless as if my mouth was stuck, and then the uncontrollable tears came. I could not stop crying; I just couldn't. I immediately felt guilty for not being able to save my friend. There were signs, but I didn't take it seriously. I felt the outcome would have been different if I had done something different. My mind was cloudy. I found the strength to leave work and go home. When I got home, tears started back. It felt unreal, and I hoped it was just a dream.

I called my friend's phone again, hoping to hear his voice on the other end. No response. I cried from the time I entered my house to the night. I cried so much that I fell asleep. I didn't even eat anything. The next day, I was scheduled for work but couldn't find the strength to go, so I called out. Tears began again; I couldn't stop crying. I felt I let my friend down and didn't hear his cry for help. I thought some of the things we discussed weren't a big deal, but it turned out they were. I blamed myself for a long time afterward. It took me a minute to get myself together.

Experiencing this sad situation opened my eyes to a lot of things. After this happened, I started to see things differently in life. I remember talking about how I went through a long depression stage in my life to my friend. It was so hard to overcome, but I prayed and prayed. It took years for me to see the light. Seeing someone so close experience the same thing but not make it out redirected my mindset, relationships, etc. You never know what a person is going through, so you must be mindful of how you treat people. Life is hard, so battling other issues can intensify it.

Real life was starting to become much more straightforward. I always had conversations with people who encouraged me not to get stuck at my job because there was more out there for me. However, I didn't want to listen at the time because I had gotten comfortable. Looking back, I regret not moving along with the internship or the opportunity to build my experience once I graduated. It took more work to maneuver in the field three years later, as most companies require a degree and at least two years of experience. I had the degree, but getting the experience was brutal. They would only hire me if I had the experience, but how could I gain the experience if they didn't hire me?

In 2018, my journey at Turner ended, I resigned, and I decided to take a leap of faith and walk away from it all. I didn't have a job lined up, but I trusted God to lead me in the right direction. I just knew it was time to leave. I completed over one hundred applications prior to this but hadn't heard anything yet. I wasn't concerned, as I planned to sit out of work for a while. However, an insider in the human resources field told me to try the temp agency months before resigning. I applied, and less than two weeks later, I interviewed for a lead-generator role.

The lead generator worked under the recruiter, so this would be the best opportunity for me to gain experience. However, I still wasn't expecting to get the job and was preparing to sit out. After my interview, they offered me the position, and no one could tell me God isn't good. When I walked away, everything began to fall into place for me. If I didn't step out on faith, I would still be there with many regrets about not moving along with my career path. After working for two months in the role, I was promoted and offered a recruiter role. It was where I was able to showcase my skills.

I was able to gain experience, attend orientation, and hire others seeking employment, among other things. I enjoyed working there and had the pleasure of meeting some lovely individuals with whom I built relationships outside of work. For instance, Joy, Cassandra, Ms. Carole, Quintina, Angel, and many more. Although I built relationships with all of them, I was closest to Cassandra. We would go to lunch together every day and were extremely close. She told me about her daughter and Sandy when I first met her. I thought Sandy was her other child, but it was her dog. She loved her dog, husband, and daughter, and her eyes always light up when discussing them.

During our time working together, Cassandra battled some health issues, but she never let that stop her from being a strong individual. One day, we had a luncheon at work, and everyone had to bring something. Cassandra brought deviled eggs, which everyone loved them. I became addicted to them and even had her make them for me on special occasions. I don't know her special ingredient(s), but, boy, was those eggs *delicious*.

A year after working there, I became pregnant with my second child. Luckily, I wasn't as sick as I was during my first pregnancy and could still work. However, there were days when I wasn't feeling well, but Cassandra and other team members looked out for me. Before going out on leave, they surprised me with a baby shower, and I was so happy. I wasn't expecting it, but having a fantastic friend like Cassandra always knew how to make me smile. And, of course, she made deviled eggs for me that day.

On December 27, 2019, my handsome son was born. It was a fantastic experience because my husband and daughter were in the room with me to comfort me beforehand. We laughed and joked around, and although I was full of medication and feeling a bit out of it, it was a lovely moment. I didn't want any more children, but my husband wanted a son. It took me a while to think about it but seeing the joy on my daughter's face at having a brother made it all worth it. She was also a big help.

When my son was just two months old, I returned to work. It was a tough day for me because I was breastfeeding and felt uncomfortable. A lot had changed, and I didn't want to be back at work. I preferred a work-from-home position. That day, I decided to resign from my job, effective immediately. It would give me the time to be home and care for my son without sending him to daycare so early. Being home was better for me. While at home, I applied to multiple work-from-home jobs, and a month later, I was hired.

Life may not always turn out the way we expect. God has a plan for all of us. No matter how hard we try to control our lives, things can be more difficult without God's guidance. Without his help, I would not be where I am today. My mission was to become successful, but my story is still going, so stay tuned. I may not be where I want to be right now, but I am thankful to God that I am not where I used to be. He has made a way for not only me but also my family. As I continue this journey called life, I pray for his guidance for all of us.

As my story unfolded, it allowed me to be in a place of healing. I used to be afraid to tell my story and show that I encountered hardships, failures, depression, and more. I didn't want others to judge me. I had to pretend I had it all together when I was falling apart. I tried to heal, but when you are fighting a battle with yourself, it makes things much harder to overcome. Although I achieved many of my dreams, there were other things that I had to work on, the biggest one being myself. I never realized how much help I needed and never thought I would seek help. I used to portray myself as perfect, but I learned it's okay to ask for help and be vulnerable.

I've hurt many people with my words and actions during my journey. I used to have an out-of-control attitude, and my mom always told me I needed to change. I didn't care about other people's feelings, and I was vicious. Even though I had a heart and feelings,

I didn't want to show it because I felt that people would betray me every time I did. I used to expect everyone around me to be perfect, whether they were friends or significant others. If they did anything wrong, I would cut them off. But who am I to put such restrictions on anyone? God forgave me repeatedly, and I'm grateful for that. What if he had given up on me?

Nowadays, I can see things much more apparent. Therapy has helped me a lot. I've wanted to overcome my past, and now I'm living in the future I prayed for. I've wanted to change my bad behavior, how I talked to people when upset, my selfishness, evilness, anger, and so on. I'm in a better place than I was. Although I still have a way to go, I thank God I'm no longer in my old state of mind. God is good. He had mercy on me and saved me.

Letter to myself

Dear self,

I am sorry for not loving you the way I should have. I caused you a lot of worry and took you through many changes. I allowed you to get stuck in a difficult place to escape. Instead of allowing you to live your best life, I just existed for a long time. I regret letting others dictate my emotions and allowing them to change who I am. If I could turn back time, I would, but since I can't, let's start a new journey together.

Starting now, I promise to love you and live my best life. I promise to forgive and let go of grudges. I promise to work on my attitude and be true to myself. I promise to prioritize taking care of you before others. I promise to ensure you are doing well in all aspects of life.

I had to make a U-turn from the old path I was on. It led me toward a dead end, complete with snakes, fake friends, drama, depression, stress, hurt, hatred, and danger. But now I am headed to victory, success, a beautiful lifestyle, and more. This new life will be great if I let God lead and take complete control, which I did already. So are you ready?

Sincerely,
Self

My story—to be continued.

In memories of the following:

Owner of Leadway
Johnnie
Grandma (mom's mother)
Mutt Dear
Cassandra
Lenny
Fluffie
Andrew
Mary Ann
Jacqueline
May their souls rest in peace until we see each other again.

ABOUT THE AUTHOR

Sharoslyn Levett Roach Benton, also known as Dana in her hometown, is a small business owner, author, and a human resources professional. She owns Scentsation Creation by Sharoslyn (SCS Selfcare), which aims to help individuals identify areas in their lives to prioritize self-care. Sharoslyn is also an advocate for breaking generational curses.

Currently residing in Decatur, Georgia, Sharoslyn is married and has two children. She enjoys spending time with her family and friends, traveling, working out, and helping others. Before getting too busy, she was the former youth ministry director at In the Bible Christian Ministry. In her role, she incorporated her creativity, art, and views with children of all ages. Sharoslyn's role models include Tyler Perry, Oprah Winfrey, Judge Lynn Toler, and her parents.

Key points

Sharoslyn always had a vision in high school to spread her wings, to become successful, and to come back to build up the community in her hometown. She didn't know where and how to start so she let fear cloud her vision. Within every position she worked in and the accomplishments she made as an adult, she soon broke free from fear and let her strength guide her. She knew this was not her end; it was only the beginning which was going to manifest into something extraordinary. In 2020, Sharoslyn knew that her calling was working with people and serving the communities by helping them break negative generational cycles. She began working on her vision by starting an organization for *breaking unhealthy generational cycles*, based off her own personal experiences through life.

Sharoslyn's vision

Her vision is to create a foundation that will provide you with the tools that in turn will help break generational patterns and prioritize self-care habits. For all people (youth and adults) who are struggling with a challenging upbringing, it's about empowering *all* to restructure and build a positive generational legacy and destroy the negative cycle.

> "You must educate yourself and build that drive because one day, you may be faced with the reality of being alone on your journey without the support of others."
>
> —Sharoslyn

www.ingramcontent.com/pod-product-compliance
Lightning Source LLC
LaVergne TN
LVHW040926131224
799040LV00009B/348